TURN & WALK

an *unexpected* quest

Carol L Babcock

TURN & WALK:
an *unexpected* quest

Copyright © 2020 Carol Babcock

All rights reserved

Turn & Walk
Publishing

P.O.Box 12741
Kansas City, Missouri 64116

ISBN 978-0-9885747-1-7 (paperback)

Contents

Foreword – Labyrinth vi
PART ONE: THE TERRAIN
    Chapter 1: Meet the Gods 1
    Chapter 2: Sweet Beginnings 16
    Chapter 3: Indoctrination 25
    Chapter 4: Stepping In 37
    Chapter 5: Rough Trail 57
PART TWO: WAYFINDING
    Chapter 6: Walk or Wait 62
    Chapter 7: Who's With Me? 76
    Chapter 8: Praying 88
    Chapter 9: Solo Trek 94
    Chapter 10: Quantum Kingdom 106
    Chapter 11: Allies 115
    Chapter 12: Prophetic Milieu 129
    Chapter 13: What About Us 142
    Chapter 14: Labyrinth Reprise 149
    Chapter 15: Released 151
    Chapter 16: Peace Talks 162
PART THREE: PEACE IN THE PASTURE
    Chapter 17: Quantum Reality 165
    Chapter 18: Hawk's View 169
    Chapter 19: Assent to Peace 177
Afterword 181
Lexicon 185

Foreword

On a clear June afternoon, I walked my first labyrinth. My whole world changed.

I'd only heard that word a couple days before on public television. They replayed a Bill Moyers' interview of a man unfamiliar to me, Joseph Campbell. Campbell had written a book about the religions of the world. He mentioned labyrinths were constructed as tools for religious practice many centuries ago but didn't explain more than that.

Intrigued about how the ancients related to God, I hunted for something local I could examine. From a primitive internet search, I found one in the description of a retreat facility twenty minutes from my house.

A winding dirt road led me to an unpainted marker. I walked toward an open area beyond the marker not knowing what to look for. I hadn't done my typical library research. All I knew was labyrinths had some sort of order, much different from mazes which are designed to puzzle and frustrate.

I came to satisfy my scientific curiosity. To see what a labyrinth actually looked like and how it functioned. I wondered why the old European religions might have used them. Why would people here in Kansas make one?

Faith was similar to science for me, not oppositional. To learn a biblical principle was only the first step in knowing. The principal had to be acted on, tested, to be believed. In the same way, to learn a house is wired with electricity is only the first step. To believe, to really know, someone must act on that belief. Flip a switch. Today was my day.

This secluded clearing is surrounded by natural timber. The quiet calm stalls me at the labyrinth entrance. The spring green grass is ankle high so I can't get a clear view of its full layout. A concrete bench sits in the center and partially visible rows of white cobble define the sides of the two-foot-wide walkway. A dilapidated birdfeeder hugs a post nearby.

One deep breath. I look down and take a step in.

I step sure. Four steps forward and the white cobble guides my steps into a left turn. Walking slowly along a quarter of the circle while surveying the path slightly in front of my toes. Just grass. I turn, reversing direction 180 degrees. I walk parallel to the first segment, toward the entrance. Another left turn. Still in that turn, I look up and see only the bench.

My body locks in position. My mind works hard to sort concrete reality from compelling perception. If God was sitting on that bench, his eyes would meet mine. I'm drenched in self-awareness. I feel small. I've never knelt before, but I feel an urge to kneel now.

My intellect argues with my soul. *It's just a trail! It's only a bench!*

But this turn, this moment, is transforming my life. In some untimed time, I complete that turn and walk the next segment. But I feel different. I sense the presence of that bench to my right. Not in a bad way, just some sort of presence, but very real.

I sense no trickery in this design. Yet so early in this experience, my original motive of simply seeking knowledge about this physical instrument is changing. Now it's a pure profound encounter. Scientific curiosity and vague hypothesis have evaporated. I'm now absorbed in my own experiment.

The early turns really challenge my mind. They turn either left or right, some 90°, most are 180°. Very straightforward. It makes no rational sense for me to feel any emotion at all, but as I walk and turn away from that bench at the center only for a moment, I feel terrible. When I turn away from the Bench, it seems like I'm turning my back on God.

"Please understand; I'm not rejecting you. I'm simply turning. I don't want to hurt you. It's the path."I'm surprised by my own timid voice.

My rational mind shakes its head but gives way to my spirit mind and this supernatural, yet distinctly real, experience.

I stand still for a long time. Both physical and spiritual aspects to this new reality settles into my heart. The location and position of the Bench does not change, only my perspective does. If that Bench represents God, then God hasn't moved. Sometimes he's to my left, sometimes to my right, but it's *my* location that changes. The emotions I feel: fear, rejection, abandonment, are legitimate, but are affected only by *my* point of view. This beautiful, brand-new truth, filled me with peace to my core.

Another turn, another grassy path. The same landscape. Same general location. A continuation of the same labyrinth walk, yet each turn and each segment of this single path is incomparable to the last. I walk slow, one small step at a time. Each footfall overflows with visual recall and emotion from decades back. Feelings long left behind – fresh.

As I tread through segments and turns, I begin to grasp the correlation between my life and this labyrinth. One labyrinth walk corresponds to one life. In life, I hadn't seen changes or challenges I walked blindly into. In this labyrinth, I didn't see turns coming, but as I walked out of each turn, my mindset, my reasoning was transformed.

At the exit, I felt a sort of joy. Peace maybe. My timeless walk through this labyrinth was an unexpected encounter. I couldn't have imagined or described a hypothesis for this grand experiment. I looked again at the whole place to capture what I learned, more accurately, what I now know.

I now know God is central to whatever life I've lived. When I made a turn, right or left, I now know I was not judged right or wrong. I now know God didn't turn his back on me nor was I evicted.

I now know God didn't reject, abandon, or condemn me during the divorce I didn't see coming. The pain I felt from all the associated losses was offset by amazing encounters of mystical reality. I now believe that I *can know* what I can't see.

This foreword is a condensed version of the detailed labyrinth experience for the reader because this book's storyline follows that pattern: turns to one side, then the other, walking forward not sure of the path ahead. An experimental journey of a person living out my best intentions to conform to paths set by others. But when that whole way of life began to crumble, I desperately stepped out hunting for answers. The stories describe a series of unexpected turns and my transformative walk into a different spiritual reality.

PART ONE – THE TERRAIN

Chapter 1: Meet the gods

High Plains Primer

Breakfast on the farm was oatmeal, cream of wheat, or pancakes and eggs (if we had chickens laying). If those options were scant, we ate boiled wheat from the barn. I remember watching it boil for twenty minutes, then chewing it for twenty minutes. I couldn't eat very much before the school bus came; it was too much work to consume, but what I did get down kept me from feeling hungry all day.

Our large garden supplied green beans and tomatoes for canning. A deep wooden bin attached to the coolest room in the basement held enough potatoes to get us through the winter. They felt softer as the winter dragged on but would be mashed or stewed. One bad potato could threaten the rest so we kept a vigilant nose. When sent to the "fruit room" for anything else, Mom expected us to hunt any rotting potato down and throw it to the chickens or pigs.

We butchered a hog in the fall. Grandpa carried off the hog's head to make souse loaf or head cheese in a clean room of the barn. Dad put a pan under the hanging carcass to catch the blood. He combined it with barley and spices and cooked it. Then he stuffed the dark mass into casings for a Czech specialty sausage. Dad always ate it with another link sausage, lighter in color and made from the same pig's head called jaternice. I could eat it with sauerkraut in equal amounts.

In the house, Mom cut up the fat into huge roasting pans and rendered it down for lard. The lard was beautiful, smooth, and white when it cooled. Roasted pork chunks were packed within the lard in to five gallon metal buckets and stored in the cool basement for winter meals. She kept the cracklings, crunchy remains of the lard rendering, in a roaster in the kitchen for several days afterward as a salty crunchy treat.

Any time we needed meat for the family of eight, plus an occasional hired hand, Dad or brother Paul would go hunt antelope, deer, or pheasant from our pastures. As a matter of fact, most of the meat we ate came off our land. Venison tasted of the sage brush eaten that day.

Mom ordered chicks from a catalog. They got their start on commercial feed, but grew up from eating vegetable peelings and grain from our fields. We kept all the hens for laying eggs but cleaned (that means butchered) the roosters at about four pounds or two months old.

Producing large amounts of food for this large family required everyone to engage, Mom organized an assembly line method for

Meet the Gods

butchering chickens. She lined us up, each kid deemed strong enough would hold one chicken, both legs in one tight grip, both wings in our other tight grip. Then she pulled the chicken's head tight and cut it off with a huge knife.

"Don't let it get away!...Hold it tight!"

When a chicken finally went limp, she'd take it from my locked hand and dip it into a deep pot of boiling water a few times. Those who have shared this experience can recall the stench of steaming feathers and blood. Those who haven't aren't missing anything of importance.

The top – maybe only – priority on the farm was producing food. Food for the whole year. I don't recall any conversation or activity that might be considered personal development. No talk of ideas or emotional topics, just basic physical survival on these barren plains.

I remember when we got electricity from town. Before this, Dad had rigged up thick glass batteries to the windmill that pumped our water. He lined them up against the walls of a stucco building he built around the legs of the tower. But technology was finally getting to our sparsely populated corner of Colorado. When the Rural Electric Association came to our county, farmers "on the hill" with us agreed to buy the pole line so electrical wire could reach our area.

Around the same time, our telephone technology changed too. From a square oak and metal ringer to a beige table-top rotary dial somewhere, but our ring remained two shorts and one long. Still on the party line, it was interesting to me to pick up the receiver and hear one of our neighbors talking in the Czech language.

When I was fourteen, a nice gray radio that sat on the dresser in our girls' bedroom. Don't remember where it came from. No matter how slowly I adjusted that dial, I could find only one station: 1520 -

KOMA, Oklahoma City, and that only after the sun went down. I strained to hear western music of the times through incessant static.

I remember we were sent to bed at 7:30 no matter how old we were, three girls in one bedroom, three boys in the other. Six kids in four beds, sharing determined by pecking order. Dad was usually gone, I guess playing cards in town. Mom settled onto the couch with a Readers' Digest and a bowl of cottage cheese. I knew how to pour just the right amount of French dressing over it so she was pleased. She'd worked hard all day so deserved to rest and read.

I didn't sleep much on the farm. Once the house was dark, I'd slip out of bed without disturbing my sisters and tiptoe downstairs. Sometimes, I'd eat cold pinto beans I'd hidden in the back of the refrigerator. Sometimes I'd fix oatmeal with brown sugar and butter, just enough for one, and clean up so no one would notice the next morning. Sometimes I'd crawl outside my bedroom window and sit on the roof looking at the Milky Way.

During daylight hours, Mom and Dad yelled. I heard their voices but couldn't make out their words. We probably didn't do something right, didn't do it fast enough, or didn't eat the fat on our plate. Dad might hit one of the boys with the back of his fist, but Mom was methodical. She used a braided leather weapon she called "the quirt". She told us often how she hated lying. And if she thought someone might be lying, she would line us up and whip us one by one until she "got the truth" out of us. The "truth" that satisfied her anyway.

I found safety in the seclusion of wild pastures. Cactus, coyotes, and rattlesnakes were at least predictable. I just walked around the cactus patches, they couldn't reach out. Coyotes roamed endlessly because they were hungry. I was not their food so just tried not to startle them when they trotted by.

Meet the Gods

Rattle snakes (diamond back) were common, and if I kept a respectful eye out for them, we would part congenial ways. I carried what we called a snake stick. Two nails were hammered into the cut off end of an old broom then the nail heads cut off. It was used to pin a snake to the ground. From the age of 6, we were taught to use it and were allowed to stay out in the pastures all day. If Mom wanted us, she would honk the car horn three times and we were each supposed to come to the top of the nearest hill so she could count heads. If that satisfied her, we could go about our wandering.

I knew nothing of God, hadn't heard of Jesus or church. But when I laid on the dry grass, the same grass the cattle ate, the ants carried off, the coyotes trotted over, I felt honestly valued – as valued a part of the universe as the critters I shared this place with, tiny or large.

I felt a part of that ground I laid on. I felt safe during those hours and days spent absorbed into the natural world around me. No harsh demands. No mean voices. No physical pain. I didn't think anyone would ever harm a piece of ground. I had not yet become aware of emotional pain.

I saw Dad a lot

When I was young, I saw him sleeping on the couch in the middle of the day as I tiptoed by. From outside the door to his shop, I saw him working on projects. He hammered things, welded things, screwed nuts and bolts on equipment. I wished I could ask him questions about his projects, but I knew it was safer in the shadows.

When he was away, I slipped in there and looked around. I dug through the nail bins for rusty ones to build my projects. And I cut wood from the scrap pile with the rusty saw. I learned to use a steel carpenter's square. I learned by watching Dad from a safe distance.

I saw Dad at supper, hunched over his plate. I saw him knock Johnny off his chair with the back of his fist. I don't remember what Johnny did. I just looked at my plate and tried hard to swallow.

I saw him duck his head and laugh as the fork Mom threw at him missed and stuck in the wall behind him, again. I think he told a joke she didn't like.

I saw Dad with animals. I saw him shoot our dog on the porch of the house. I don't know what the dog did, but he killed it to teach us kids some sort of lesson. I saw him butcher pigs, deer, and antelope for us to eat. I saw him catch and tame a magpie. He cut the skin web under the bird's tongue and taught it to say words like "hello".

I saw Dad at Louie's bar in town when I was in high school, smiling at his hand of Hearts. Only Louie and three other men there, one smoke-encrusted light bulb hung above their card table. I'd played flute with the band at the football game earlier and was getting warm near Louie's pot-bellied stove. We'd head home sometime after my brothers got changed from their football uniforms.

I saw Dad on the couch at a strange woman's house. They were "busy" so I smashed his windshield with a sledgehammer I had with me. I saw Dad with her again at the county fair carnival rides. I think he told me her name but he didn't mention his windshield. I think they made a kid.

The last time I saw Dad he was an old man, tobacco drool oozed from the side of his perpetual smirk and dropped on his shirt. His physical filth matched his mental vulgarity.

After he died, I saw pictures of Dad in an album my cousin put together. A yellowed newspaper article said he flew a T-34 airplane and crashed it in the 1949 blizzard. I saw a picture of him as a young man riding a horse upside-down like a trick rider. Pictures of him with men from Denver who came to our farm to hunt: pheasant, antelope, deer, coyotes, anything. I saw lots of pictures of dead game in laid out or hung in long rows.

I saw Dad smile in most of those pictures. Two pictures where he and Mom posed with all six of us kids, he wasn't smiling. Neither was Mom.

I liked the pictures in the album. They altered my perspective, opened up my mind to the possibility of considering other stories about him than those Mom told. I began to see Dad in a slightly brighter light.

As I closed in on my own 60s and assessed my own choices, good and bad, I wondered what pressures Dad made his choices under. What might his life be like if his soul had been acknowledged? And all that hunting; what was he truly hunting?

Over the years, I've heard hundreds of folks tenderly share comparisons of their fathers to God. Even as sentimental as those questions are, I never, ever, confused the two.

For the love of Mom

Mom commanded her world with the power of a king. "What I say goes." The symbols of her kingdom were bright naturally red wavy hair worn like a crown, and the freckles and volatile temper she claimed came with it.

And like any good king, I imagine, the provision of food ensured our loyalty. Mom maintained a fruit cellar neatly packed with jars of canned meat, pickles, fruits, and vegetables. I don't know if she was a particularly good cook, we didn't measure by a standard of flare or technique. She cooked enough good food to feed eight to ten people three times every day and made that happen from very limited resources.

Judgment. If something or someone needed to be evaluated, Mom measured by her own high expectations. Cutting remarks continually flowed from her overworked internal judge. Condemnation had little connection to evidence that I could see, but I figured she was a lot smarter than any of us.

The quirt. She enforced her judgments with a leather version of her scepter, her rod and staff. I never deduced a solid connection between the severity of crime with the severity of punishment. Each "crime" brought the same inevitable consequence.

One time, our little sister stuffed a half-eaten sandwich behind some books on the bookcase. When Mom found it days later, she lined us up in order of age and began to swing. We didn't want to get hit or let Mom hit our baby sister, so we covered for her. We all got hit.

To make a quirt (I don't want to think about why you might want to do that), take three strands of quarter-inch thick leather four feet long and fold them in half. Braid them together in the middle so you have a folded handle at one end and six separate straps at the other. Tie a knot in each strand. Don't use it on any living thing, child or critter. We hid it often, but that only increased her rage.

I was learning to relate to Mom like the people of ancient times related to their mysterious gods. That sense of duty to appease became my normal response to life, especially with people I considered authorities like Mom. I never considered whether I was happy or not, or if the gods' thinking was fair or right. I just assumed they knew better than me, had more power than me, so my only job was to make their life better.

Meet the Gods

I looked to Mom for advocacy. Found none. Hoped for affection. Nope. She stroked the yard cats but not her children. Any acceptance or encouragement from her? She made it clear most of us were never good enough, and certainly none could match her perfection.

Mom's mood was unpredictable to me. She didn't explain any pressures of life she may have felt; she didn't explain anything. And it was certainly none of my business – as her kid. She wielded the power in our world and I dare not question her – ever. I wasn't yet aware of any personal power I might have. I just had to comply as best I could with what she ordered without challenging her logic.

But I loved Mom. She taught me everything I needed to know.

She taught me to cook. Sat me on the counter, folded my hand around a long wooden spoon and said, "Stir this." That was her complete instruction for gravy. She probably assumed I would pick up on the rest by watching her as I stirred.

Mom spoke in slogans - indisputable slogans. Important slogans. Any guidance for life would come in the form of slogans. Slogans delivered without explanation left me to guess that their context must explain their meaning. However, my contextual conclusions mostly proved wrong.

"Don't you cry or I'll give you something to cry about." This meant suck it up or choke it down, but don't express emotion.

"Kids are to be seen and not heard." I got that one. Speak only when directed and only to give her an answer she approved of.

"Do what I say, not what I do." Just do what she said; don't ask why or attempt negotiating.

"Work gets done with elbow grease." Try harder. If that doesn't work, try harder.

Mom taught me not trust what anyone else said. "Don't believe anything you hear and only half of what you see." She was the exception to that rule. What came out of her was to be accepted as absolute truth. If I heard anything that contradicted her, I trained myself to override it with Mom's truth.

Propaganda. She told me what to see - even when I didn't see what she told me. My mind made her truth override visual facts. She told me how to feel. When she told me the house was warm enough, I tried to feel warmer.

Mom taught me prejudice. The boys in the family especially the ones with hazel eyes like hers and her brothers were favored. They had privilege and position. We fought, like kids do, and when I got punched in the face and gut, I scratched back. My nails got clipped down to the quick; the boys got no consequences. She taught me I had no power because of her own prejudices of gender and ethnicity. Because of my dark brown eyes, hair and deep tan, I was a "dirty little Bohunk."

Mom taught me that people hurt. Not only do they hurt but they hurt others. She called me a dirty Bohunk because I looked like my dad's Bohemian (Czech) people. Maybe she was hurt, or mad at Dad; she was always mad at Dad.

Mom taught me to not expect touch. She never voluntarily touched me. I don't remember her even brushing my hair, my sister Teena did. Don't recall ever seeing her hold any of my siblings. I've tried to recall any loving words or touch from either parent but came up empty.

Meet the Gods

When I was sixteen, I had my first headache. I caught Mom sitting in the big oak rocking chair and asked if I could sit on her lap.

"What do you want to do that for?"

"I know this headache will go away if I could put my head on your shoulder."

She didn't say no so I sat down, put my arms around her, and placed my forehead on her collarbone area. She didn't move her hands from the arms of the chair. Didn't say a word. I stayed there for a minute, then told her thank you and left to try something different.

Mom taught me not to expect anyone to love me. As I watched other girls from high school begin dating, I worked up enough nerve to ask her, "Will anyone ever want me?"

"Beauty is in the eyes of the beholder," she said. I didn't know what she meant by that and didn't dwell on it.

She trained me to not ask questions. One time, I ventured, "Can I ask you something?"

"I don't answer stupid questions." It probably was, so I stopped asking.

All those locked-up questions built-up, however, and spilled out years later.

Mom taught me abandonment and rejection. I heard all her painful stories told from a victim's perspective.

A short history of Mom – as told by Mom. Born sixth of nine kids. Felt ignored after she was about five and figured it was because she wasn't cute anymore. Molested by her brother when she was twelve or thirteen. Condemned by her mom for wearing makeup when she was thirteen. She first ran away when she was thirteen, and often after that. Her older brothers went off to war so her mom worried about them all the time. No one worried about her.

She graduated high school when she was sixteen, but details of her story changed years later with different family audiences. She loved to read so would take a book to the bathroom at the school and read in a stall all day. She also said she ran away from home and stayed with farm families to care for their kids and clean. These story lines didn't always match up. I didn't see it as a pattern of lies; just assumed it was bravado, like exaggerating the length of a fish that got away.

Dad hit her first right after their wedding. Or, Dad didn't hit her until fourteen years into their marriage. She stated both opposing 'truths' at different times, each version delivered with the same intense scowl to drive her point home.

It pained me to listen to her stories, but I listened attentively with respect. Every time.

I wished someone could have interpreted what was going on during those early years. I took Mom at her word; I took everyone at their word. Why wouldn't I? I didn't have anything to compare with - no community to look to for models. No social interaction with others my age I could talk with to see if their lives were like mine.

This absence of conversation kept me from understanding how to think about the things of life. I was trained to expect impersonal, detached authority. Trained to be self-sufficient, make do with what I could rummage, not ask for help, and surely not ask for love.

Meet the Gods

Up and Away

The Navy recruiter came to our school in late October of my senior year. He simply stated their catch phrase, "Join the Navy and see the world," and I signed papers to enlist. I'd leave for boot camp in June after graduation. It never occurred to me to talk it out with anyone. I had just turned eighteen and Mom had clearly stated her policy on kids.

"When you're 18, you leave home. You can always come back to visit, but you have to leave."

I'd rarely gotten off the farm at all until six weeks before when Mom married Bob, a sweet, hard-working cowboy. The day they got married at the county courthouse, Dad held a pistol at me and took over our grocery store. Seemed like a good time to leave so Mom, Bob, and I began driving from Northeastern Colorado to Olympia, Washington to collect the four younger siblings from Mom's brother's home.

We traveled north, then west across the upper plains to Washington State, feeling free and happy. On the return drive, we looked for ranch jobs for Bob. I tracked our route by keeping a list of town names in pencil in a spiral notebook. When I settled in a new school in western Nebraska that September, I marked those locations on a paper map. In three weeks' time, we'd traveled across six states, thousands of miles, and seen a lot of wonderful country. However, I realized what a small piece of the whole globe I'd really seen, a tiny trail. There was so much more!

See the world? I was curious and now eager for even more.

A place sleep and food to live was all I needed and the Navy guy told me they'd provide that. The paycheck, undefined but understood, didn't intrigue me. Money had no meaning on the farm; I never heard one conversation about it. The fascination for me was an adventure into the unknown world with surety of room and board wherever I landed.

I had no concerns about the enlistment obligation. Personal choice had not yet entered my reality so I didn't consider changing my mind even after I signed. I gave my word I'd serve loyally throughout the next four years.

Nothing troubled me about serving. I knew I could work hard and do as I was told; I'd done that my whole life. Instructions from parents was nil to this point, so I simply thought I could handle any challenges of the next stage of life the same way. I'd figure it out.

When I got home from school that October day, I showed Mom the paper I'd signed. She said, "Well, I guess you're old enough. It's too late now anyway."

I graduated in May with four As, one B, and one C. Mom told me to volunteer at a nursing home until my report date, so I did. On June 11, 1971, I left home for my great adventure. Me and my little tote bag of underwear flew on an airplane from Scottsbluff to Denver. A recruiter gathered me with others and took us to the Brown Derby hotel. Next day, I had a physical exam, flew on another plane to Maryland, then followed the person in uniform with a sign to a bus that drove a bunch of us to Bainbridge. I didn't talk to anyone.

The next ten weeks of boot camp were easy. The Navy gave me blue clothes and black shoes. Marching was fun and I already knew how to make military corners on my bunk, knew how to iron my uniform, and knew how to listen. Simple. But some girls didn't stick. One girl cut herself bad. Some girls sassed back. I didn't understand. Rules and expectations were clearly stated.

Toward the final weeks, I met with a sort of career counselor. He discussed test scores with me and asked what category I intended to work in. It was the early 70s; therefore, the only work options I knew of were teaching, nursing, and secretary. Teaching required college, and I couldn't type, so I said nursing. He told me nurses are assigned to one base for the whole four years and that my scores were high enough to qualify for aviation. I smiled bigger and bigger as we talked about planes. I told him my dad was a pilot. Imagine – me, a girl, in aviation!

I spent the next eighteen months near Memphis, Tennessee in aviation electronics school. After completion of that training, I moved to California, just south of San Francisco, assigned to an antisubmarine patrol training squadron. Over the next months, I learned how to qualify as air crew on P-3 Orion turboprop planes and volunteered for as many flights as I could.

Again, the joy of those Navy years was so much more than seeing the world, which I did. I enjoyed peace of mind and freedom. I knew the structure, my duties were clear. And when my obligation, my work, my duty was completed, I was free to explore. On the farm, I never knew the rules. Tasks were assigned randomly. Never knew when, or if, I was finished or whether I had met unspoken expectations.

The military was my boss, my job, my commitment. But unlike my mother, the Navy was not my god. I could exercise compliance with the Navy's system of rules because it was a logical system focused on a clear mission. Mom's world functioned via her system of moods and preferences I could not figure out. I couldn't deduce any pattern of cause and effect within her realm. That mystery maintained her position on a pedestal for me.

Chapter 2: Sweet Beginnings

Coming Together

On the morning of 9 February, 1973, two VP-31 planes were scheduled for extended training missions westbound over the Pacific. I was thrilled to be heading to Japan, and my friend Perkins' plane heading to Guam. After I completed my preflight, I went over to wish him fair winds. Three of us were standing together in the fuselage when Perkins introduced us.

"This is Babcock. He just got orders to VP-46; I got orders to VP-40." Both had just finished Radioman school.

He couldn't have been more perfect. Hazel eyes, broad shoulders, and muscular forearms. He had dark blond hair trimmed short around his ears but with a sun-bleached longer top that he swooped to one side with a flick of his head. He stood about 5 foot 10 inches tall.

"Hi Babcock" I reached out for a solid handshake then returned to my plane.

An ordinary flight. An ordinary day – until later.

Both VP (fixed wing patrol) squadrons were stationed at Moffett Field Naval Air Station located between San Jose and San Francisco,

Sweet Beginnings

California. Three massive hangars that once housed hydrogen blimps dominated the base, but now accommodated squadrons of P3 Orion aircraft. NASA's U-2 jet glider and other rare test aircraft shared the long airstrip at the south end of San Francisco Bay.

I'd arrived a few months earlier after completing avionics school near Memphis, Tennessee. I'd been ordered in to work on a closed-circuit television system which hadn't yet been installed. Recalling the recruiter's promise of "Join the Navy and See the World" and having some spare time, I set about learning how to qualify as a flight crew member. Most flights were touch and go practice for pilots at nearby airbases and mock submarine hunting flights just off the coast.

My duties included getting the interior of the plane ready, checking the life vests, head gear, and all else for a minimum crew of nine. Securing anything loose that might turn into a projectile in flight. Training missions lasted six to ten hours, so another preflight task might include getting coffee, and sometimes lunches, from the base mess hall.

After everyone was inside, I'd pull the 13-foot ladder up into the plane, secure it, and close the door. Helmet on, strapped in, report to the cockpit, "Condition five set". My job in-flight, Observer, was to look out my little bubble window and pay attention to every minute detail of the glorious blue sky, stunning coastline, and magnificent glistening ocean. I paid close attention but the time in flight seemed timeless.

Post flight, I cleaned and organized inside of the plane, removed the 3-foot tall coffee can shaped urinal and emptied it in the hangar's head (men's bathroom). After I was finished and released by the flight engineer, I could finally go to the bathroom myself and go home. Cleaning the plane and emptying the boys' urinal was a small price to pay for the privilege to fly.

I loved this life! It was bliss to fly. My intent, as a sailor and crew member, was to earn the right to fly. It was never to get recognition as a female. I saw much of the world from these rear-facing seats. That was bliss — and a taste of heaven.

My flight this day landed on Midway Island to stay overnight, then go on to the Navy's base at Iwakuni, Japan. Midway Island had no females or barracks for them, so one of the local sailors showed me to the officers' quarters. The room was Navy-gray concrete block with a single twin bed. I hit the head (bathroom), stowed my bag appropriately, and proceeded to the Enlisted Men's club. I had to locate my crew and find out exactly when preflight would be next day; many flights took off at "zero dark-thirty".

Even though it was February, the air was damp and heavy. I wore jeans and tee shirt under my olive green flight suit and felt damp and sticky clear through. Different from the high desert climate I'd grown up in. The sun was low in the western sky but still plenty light to venture to wherever I might find the club. No information, no map, but no problem.

I enjoyed interacting with a few of the thousands of black-footed albatross, called gooney birds by locals, whose nests peppered the island. Babies were still fuzzy but larger than their mothers; the most ungraceful fascinating fowl I'd ever seen.

When I found the enlisted club, three of my crew members were sitting around a big round table beginning a card game of Spades. I was surprised to see Perkins and Babcock at the table with them. Their plane had engine trouble, landed on Midway, and would now wait for repairs.

Sweet Beginnings

A dozen sailors in aviation green flight suits gathered around the table, half in the booth, half on chairs pulled near to it. Drinking beers and telling sea stories was standard behavior, basic camaraderie of military personnel. I found an empty chair and sat down to listen. I learned preflight would be at 0330, but stayed and enjoyed more stories and laughter before noticing it was 2700 (9:00 pm).

It was dark outside now and I didn't want to get lost on the way back.

"Hey Perky, walk me back to the BQ, will ya?"

He said "I'm not ready to go yet but Babcock will. He's a good guy." Nodding toward the guy he'd introduced earlier.

I had noticed that Babcock hadn't smoked or cussed and drank straight Coke, so I agreed, and with a mutual nod, we began walking.

Two strangers walked and talked…and walked…and talked. We began in the usual Navy way with, "Where are you from?"

But neither of us knew where we were going. Buildings had very few lights and were mostly covered by trees and brush. We walked along asphalt paths until we ended up on the north beach. The sugar-white sand of the northwestern coast of the island shined bright, even though the moon was just a sliver. Our conversation turned to amazement as we shared what each of us knew about the Battle of Midway. So many military guys died right here. These beaches probably had blood and metal debris all over them. How cruel man can be to man. Ships were still under that beautiful green-blue sea.

We climbed an old wooden lookout tower to get a better perspective. The water appeared shallow for a long way out. Waves broke on a reef a few hundred feet out from the beach. The expanse of ocean and luminous sky contributed to the night. Our discussion turned to those stars overhead.

Their brilliance had no competition for thousands of miles. Both of us landlubbers pointed to constellations we recognized; I was standing just in front of him.

"There's Orion!" I pointed to the Orion constellation that our planes were named for.

He put his hands on my shoulders, turned me around and kissed me. One long kiss. Not forceful. Just holding. He had nice arms; strong arms. Good kiss.

I got nervous about preflight and he checked his watch. It was already three o'clock. We sort of marched to my quarters, said goodnight. Back in military mode, no kiss.

I met the crew, completed my tasks, and flew on to Japan. Bought my mom a set of Noritake china and myself a Kamado pot, a sort of clay grill. Took an adventure by train and loaded my goods onto the plane for home a couple days later.

When I landed back at Moffett, Babcock was right there at the plane. His flight had come back home after necessary repairs. He helped me unload my Asian treasures and followed me back to my apartment off base.

We saw each other every day after that. He would come over for breakfast before we had to report. I enjoyed cooking again. When I had my guy friends over for a card party, he came, sat off to the side and made sure that he was the last sailor to leave.

Up to this point, religion had not entered my mind. I'd never heard of God or Jesus. I knew there was a Lutheran building in the town near our farm, but thought that meant they were German people that had a club, sort of like the VFW or Grange.

My brand new friend asked me to go to church with him. We went on Sunday mornings, Sunday and Wednesday evenings. He told me all the questions in life could be answered by this book he called bible. A few weeks farther along, eight to be exact, one of the elders of his church, Clyde Elmer, and his wife, stayed after Wednesday class and sat in the pew with me. At the end of that chat, Clyde asked if I believed Jesus was the son of God.

"Well, we just read that didn't we, so, of course." I said. The three of them got really happy. I was baptized that night in a large tub in a back room of their church.

Getting Closer

After that, we began to get more physically intimate. We kissed and made out, but more frequently wrestled and played in the park. Didn't go on dates or to movies. I didn't know much about that anyway. We just spent a lot of nonworking time together.

One day, while playing leapfrog in a park, we paused to catch our breath on a bench. Panting, he said, "What would you say if I asked you to marry me?"

Leaning forward, elbows on my knees, looking at the grass, I said, "I'd probably say yes."

"Well?" He looked at her.

I turned to look at his face. "Yes."

We jumped up and down and hugged each other and ran around the park some more. Then went back to the apartment where he lived with two other sailors to share the news. This was two and a half months after we'd been introduced.

The next weeks were filled with demanding workdays and making arrangements for a wedding.

We reserved the base chapel and chaplain for Saturday, the 9th of June. There were 20 weddings already scheduled for that day. Ours would begin at 1000 hours (military time), last ten minutes, and cost $15.00.

I'd only been to one wedding before, my older sister's shotgun, so didn't know much about them. I knew I had to have a dress, rings, cake, and a party afterward for people who attend.

I bought a plane ticket for my thirteen-year-old little sister to come help and be my maid of honor. Found some pretty orange fabric for her dress, a nice princess-style pattern, and white daisy bric-a-brac for trim and to tie in her long brown hair. She was gorgeous.

The bride's dress was a nice princess pattern too. White satin with an over-skirt of lace scalloped down the front. My headdress was a big bow made from left-over satin fabric stitched to a hair comb and enough toile to bring forward over my face. I bought new white sandals with a one-inch heel.

Our song was "I'll give you a Daisy a Day" so we found a place to buy a dozen Shasta daisies and Kelley tied them together with some satin ribbon for a bouquet.

Sweet Beginnings

The groom's short task list included reserving the chapel and Chaplain Barger, putting in a military request chit for two days leave, and picking up the rings from the ring store.

Both rings were single bands of white gold with ridges etched away from a narrow black groove in the center. My ring had a single diamond sticking up from the base. $395 total; I still have the receipt. Simple designs for simple people.

The place he lived was typical of central California in the 1970s. Standard patio apartments with brilliant white rock landscaping the courtyard. He arranged for us to rent an apartment in their complex beginning the first of June. I lived in the WAVE barracks on base to save money, but I and little sister, Kelley, stayed at the apartment and sewed our dresses up until wedding day.

Our wedding color was orange, so we baked and stacked two 9 x 13 cakes, and decorated them with orange frosting. I bought two rolls of orange crepe paper and Kelley draped it from the light fixture above the dining room table.

Larry's best man and roommate, Dave, both wore their dress blue (wool) uniforms. My favorite uncle, Tom, flew up that morning and good friends, Carl and Darlene, picked him up in San Francisco.

The wedding went well. Lasted less than ten minutes. Twelve people attended: friends, a couple from church, and my Lieutenant boss. Photomate First Class and friend, Leo, took pictures. I don't remember anything the chaplain said but he had beautiful handwriting.

At the reception, Uncle Tom asked where we were going on our honeymoon. I couldn't answer. I didn't know exactly what a honeymoon was. He gave me $50 and suggested we spend it on a nice room in San Francisco.

We both had to be at work Monday, so we drove the 32 miles to San Francisco, bought a night in the Travel Lodge for $36, two corn dogs, a Coke, Orange Julius, box of crackers, and an apple and still had enough left to ride the trolley to Lombard street and Coit Tower.

I wish I had paid attention to what the chaplain said that day. It has come back to bite me thousands of times since. Something about obedience. I had no experience with what I'd just gotten myself into. I knew we'd make beautiful babies. He was a nice guy and would never hit me.

He deployed to Japan three weeks after the wedding. He was gone six months – we'd only known each four. February 9th to June 9th.

Chapter 3: Indoctrination

Rules of the Road

The marriage had rules but no one told me what they were. There was no orientation. No conversation. I only found out after I broke one. I could tell by his cold shoulder. In the early years – by that I mean the first twenty or so - I'd ask for some clarity.

Why don't we have what other couples have? What is wrong? Why don't you talk to me or tell me what to do?

His response, "You knew what you were getting into."

That always made me feel stupid. It also shut me up. I would crawl out of the room, sad and stupid, and build a list of what I might do to figure it out.

Seven days after the wedding, we went to church as a married couple for the first time. He drew a 2-inch wide line on the pew with his thumb and forefinger and made me scoot away from him. He considered any touching a public display of affection, called it PDA. We would not do PDA. First rule of the marriage. A rule that wasn't there before. We held hands and I snuggled up close to his side three times a week before the wedding.

He hugged other women at church in greeting, even some men, but not me, his wife. Not at church; not at home. I didn't, and still don't understand, but did my best to comply. I occasionally saw other couples touching, but if I slipped my arm into his while standing or walking together, he'd pull away, leaving me embarrassed and feeling dirty somehow.

Once a year we took long car trips from California to Texas, he would describe how church people behave in the True Church. He didn't go as deep as I hoped, but always ended these conversations with the authority of, "Babcock Chapter 5 verse 7" he'd joke. He wasn't referring to himself, but his mother.

One church rule that came up often was women being silent. Church classes pointed to a particular bible verse telling us women if we had questions, we were to ask our husbands at home. When I did ask at home, he'd say, "You're a Christian. You should know."

Decades later, I learned this Catch 22, this circular reasoning, came from the Texas Bible Belt culture he was raised in. He conformed to his social environment like I conformed to laws of nature on the rural plains.

He left for deployment in Japan three weeks after we were married. During the six month periods he was overseas, I dug into the bible studies of his church. One older woman, Phoebe, commented in class as an answer to some question, "Well, we all know what the Philistines did to the Israelites." I didn't even know what a Philistine or an Israelite was, let alone what they did. I felt just too stupid so I left and never went back to that little bunch of fourteen heaven-bound saints.

Indoctrination

A month before he came home from deployment, I began attending a large congregation of over 100. This one had bible studies in the Old Testament on Wednesday nights and the New Testament on Sunday mornings. They didn't believe in having food in the building, children's homes, or missionary organizations, but they accepted me and my many questions.

Trying Harder

When we married, of course I was aware that I'd married his family too. But I didn't realize his church was as much his family as his mother and father. Church of Christ culture ran deep in his blood.

After our enlistments were up in 1976, we moved from California to Nebraska and he got work at a sprinkler irrigation company within two weeks. He understood his responsibility to provide for his growing family meant getting and keeping a job. We had our first baby boy three years in to the marriage, followed eighteen months later by our second.

After he changed jobs, we began to move from town to town along the Burlington Northern Railroad line in western Nebraska and Wyoming. He'd let me know we needed to move and I'd make arrangements. Contacting a hauler to pull our trailer house, closing utilities, starting new ones at the next location I'd not yet seen. I'd get a phone book and get to work. His work was keeping his job, mine was everything else.

With every move, my first task after hooking up utilities was to locate a Church of Christ to lock in to. No matter the size or distance away, that was the only denomination he would consider. No musical instruments, no steeple on the building, and in many locations, no food in the building, no support of mission work or orphanages, and communion twice every Sunday.

Each congregation claimed themselves as the only Christians doing things God's perfect way. Keeping the Church pure seemed the primary goal. Each held bible study sessions Sunday morning, Sunday and Wednesday evening. Everyone carried a well-worn Bible thick with concordances and comments sections.

I assumed the men who taught bible classes had some degree of bible scholarship. I'd come to know the deacons and elders of the church in Sunnyvale, California, and had seen them read and research for hours between classes they taught. I assumed the men in the Midwest were as dedicated and serious.

The role of women in this culture didn't make sense to me - ever. It was a popular topic for preachers but seemed to be preached and taught for the purpose of keeping us in our place. And repeated the theme that men were to be the head of the household like Jesus is the head of the church. A declaration without discussion.

Church leaders told me how to live. I'd be right with God if I obeyed. Life would be good if I was baptized and lived like them. I kept living as though what they said was true, not considering that information was wrong, and not experiencing any evidence of what they told me.

Whatever new place we moved to, I sought answers to issues that were illogical to me. Why not use pianos or guitars during worship service? Many of the tiny churches we attended only had two or three men, and some needed help to carry the tune. Instrumental music was such a sin that my mother-in-law told my three-year-old daughter she would go to hell if she listened to Christian songs on the radio.

Indoctrination

Why aren't women allowed to pray? Or pass the trays of grape juice and crackers offered weekly as part of worship? Why are we taught women are to keep silent in church? Why do women, even women with a degree in childhood education have to operate under the authority of a man, regardless of how inept he might be?

Several illogical and hurtful events happened throughout the 1980s and 1990s. One youth minister was let go because he let teenage girls pray aloud in a circle of teens in his home. I was told to quit teaching a Bible class in the middle of a session. A rambunctious group of thirteen boys and two girls, ages between 11 and 13.

Shortly after three of those young boys got baptized, one of the deacons dismissed me, stating it was not right that a woman should be teaching men, and that these three baptized boys were now men.

No one else picked up that class. My own two sons were in that class. I asked my husband to take over the class, I'd even prepare the material for him. I thought I could be supportive but he refused. I felt so undercut and helpless. No teaching at church or at home any more.

Many things I didn't understand just had to be set aside. I truly believed the best about men. As a woman in the Navy, officers and enlisted men in authority over me consistently lead with the greater good as their target. No experience compelled me to think otherwise. I assumed men in leadership of the church had God's best in their minds, I assumed they understood God's system.

I didn't yet know God's method.

Fifty ways to kill a marriage.

In 2004, Oprah Winfrey interviewed author, Greg Behrendt, about his book, He's Just Not That In to You. I listened passively while I swept floors and folded clothes that afternoon. I stopped, sat on the couch and cried. Every single trait they talked about I recognized. We'd been married thirty years and I realized in that hour, he'd never been "in to me."

To resolve my tears, I wrote a long list. A Paul Simon tune, Fifty Ways to Leave Your Lover, came to my mind. It offered a way to understand how I'd been treated: fifty ways to kill a marriage.

Why would someone stay married to a person who dislikes them, marginalizes them, devalues and overpowers everything she does toward growing together? Why did I? Because I loved him.

My hands shook as I wrote. Awareness, vivid memories, and resentment burned through my body.

The Commodore 64 Affair

1983 – We'd been married ten years and relocated eight times. Larry's work territory was a four hundred mile stretch mostly west of the town of McCook, Nebraska, and he stayed away from home five or six days a week. I wasn't allowed to know where he was staying, and he let me know he wouldn't be calling me.

"What if something happens?"

Indoctrination

"You can call the railroad. They'll know where I am."

He didn't tell me who to call so I assumed I should already know (stupid me), so I didn't ask.

I pinched pennies hard during those years. He stayed in hotels with Jacuzzi tubs along the railroad lines in Nebraska and Colorado and ate steak dinners on company expense. The boys and I ate bologna at home. We got hand-me-down clothes from their older cousins, Brady and Brant, a couple times a year. I burned wood to heat the house and keep gas bills down. The meter reader came to verify one January because the bill was only $19.00. I felt good about that.

The absurdity of the situation was that when he came home, he brought parts and accessories to a Commodore 64 computer. He spent a total of $3200 on that black and white assemblage of primitive components: a monitor, keyboard, hard drive, and dot-matrix printer. And he spent his weekend time at home learning how to write "if. . . then" statements so the thing could show a math problem, 2+2 = 4 on the monitor.

I was pregnant with our third child; the boys were ages 5 and 7. He was out of town and out of contact Monday through Friday. I missed him. When he did come home, he didn't ask about the boys or me, he only talked about this new hobby. He had set up a desk using an old door in the windowless spare bedroom in the basement. Somehow, he reasoned, this computer activity equipped him for a job promotion. He fixed railroad signals, electronics. Computer programming would be the coming thing. This was his justification for ignoring us.

But I loved him.

He was my white knight all week -- week after week. I wanted him to be happy. If buying a commodore 64 made him happy, I'd make do on whatever was left. I sat my pregnant body on the bed behind him, waiting and loving the back of his head. He looked at white text on a black screen. The boys played in the living room. His laundry from the past week jostled in the washing machine just outside that dark room.

I wished he would turn around and talk to me - or just talk to me. I wondered where he'd worked all week. Wondered what people he'd worked with all week. Wondered what interesting things he'd eaten all week.

Sunday after church, he napped while I ironed his shirts and packed his bag for the next week – and cried. I hugged his soft socks and coupled them up. Folded his shirts so the collars wouldn't roll. If someone was looking to promote him, they sure wouldn't mark him down because of his wrinkled shirts.

He wouldn't engage in conversation involving cash flow either. Just told me how much to give the church, without ever looking at the checkbook. We gave $60 a week to the church, and sent $75 a month to his brother, a missionary in Uganda, Africa. I kept grocery spending under $80 per month for the three of us who lived there. Our house payment was high, $634; those were the days of 13% interest on mortgages.

The church in McCook loved the kids and me. Our friends from church, Mike and Karon, gave us scraps of red and black paisley carpet to glue onto our basement floor. They could afford to have new carpet installed and I was grateful for that layer of rubber and fabric over the concrete. I made myself a maternity tent-dress from dark brown double-knit fabric brought in a bag of clothes. Made bloomers from black and white striped feather-ticking for warmth. Reworked a couple worn-out men's cowboy shirts into pajamas for the boys. I kept the western cut of the upper back and the snap closure and repurposed the excess fabric into footies. My little boys

Indoctrination

looked good in their flannel one-piece plaid pajamas – and they were warm in this cold house.

I was still in love with my white-knight husband, but it hurt to be so poor. Larry was the man of the house; he did what he did without challenge from me. I knew if I asked why, he'd stay gone longer. I was carrying our third baby and raising two young sons and felt totally alone. I felt I had all the responsibility of caring for this family without any voice or power.

But I loved him.

I loved his back, his broad shoulders, I wanted to make love to him. In the night, I snuggled up next to him, slid my hand over his back, over his waist, and waited. If he allowed my hand to stay, I snuggled closer, and hoped.

He was in every thought during my days. What would Larry want me to do?

I sang love songs to him all week long, but he wasn't there.

I loved him.

Every two weeks, he brought his pay stub home and I did the math verifying deductions. One time, I noticed the $6.00 line item for my life Insurance was not there. Two weeks later, I looked for it specifically. Not there. When I got a chance to talk to him, I mentioned that the railroad made some kind of mistake and the allotment for my life insurance payment was not there.

He said, "I canceled it."

My head spun. I'm sure I looked confused but still asked the forbidden question, "Why?"

"You're not the bread winner."

"But the kids are still young! What will you do if I died? Even a house cleaner and babysitter would cost you $20,000."

At church, we had seen a chart describing the worth of a wife so my mind had clung to that information. I knew if I didn't earn my keep, he could discard me.

He walked away.

I felt worthless again. So, so, so many times over these decades I'd been put in my place, a marginalized place. Again, I felt like a zero. Even though he spoke in polite tones, I still felt the slice of his words.

But I loved him.

He never introduced me by my name. If we stood in a circle and introductions were made, he would say "this is my wife." No additional surname or descriptive affectionate name even as trite at 'my better or other half' - nothing. He treated every woman at church more cordial than me. Hugging and laughing with them. I found myself joining their circle just to be close to him. He even asked me if I could try to be more like Pat or Debbie but wouldn't tell me how to do that.

If we walked somewhere, I'd slide my hand gently into the open space of his bent elbow like I'd seen other couples do. He would pull his arm up and away. I was embarrassed, he wasn't. Then he'd joke that in Japan, the wife walks three steps behind the husband.

But I loved him.

Indoctrination

Every time I had an idea, he shot it down. I had ideas all the time, there were always problems to be solved. In the middle of my first sentence, he'd say, "No."

"No what?"

"No to whatever you're asking for."

I was constantly disappointed, let down, and discouraged. What's so sad is that I still tried.

But I loved him.

Or maybe, I loved the thought of love. I felt affection. I hungered for intimate philosophical conversation.

He showed affection - until we got married. We had long deep conversations - until we got married. I had not experienced either up to that point so when hope showed up at the proposal of marriage, I fell into it, only to have the door slammed at "I do."

He was nice and polite. Everyone at church liked him. But polite self-control didn't change his message. He put me and the kids on the back burner -- behind work, church, and television, in that order.

I don't think the kids had any idea how many hundreds of times I begged him to come home from work to attend a school or family function. They had no idea how hard it was to get him to simply agree to be in a photo. I took pictures whenever possible to capture the memory because it was so rare.

Finally, I changed some things. I began referring to him as my friend. I stopped wearing the wedding ring; I couldn't honestly wear it any longer. It's not that I fell out of love; it was more that he gave me nothing *to* love. He didn't hit me or yell at me, but was passive and self-satisfied, leaving me nothing to connect to. Over the decades, I just wore out from rejection and abandonment. He continued to do the things that starved it to death years ago.

This prayer is from my journal:

God, how do I live with this? What to do about this sadness. It's so sad God. Is there something wrong with me that I long for the arms of a man who loves me? Why am I joined in marriage with a man who doesn't? All these memories flood forward. I hunger for a face with eyes that look into mine with affection and understanding. Was this not meant to be? Did I make the wrong choice? I know it's my fault but don't know what I could have done different. Did I develop it wrong? Was it wrong to expect love when that was not his intent? Did I marry and join my life with a cripple who didn't look like a cripple?

Nothing about our marriage got better over time. I should have let it all go – over and over and over and over. But he made me so crazy mad. Smiling, then delivering cutting words with a kind tone that's supposed to cover all the crap he just dished out. My head spun often - with hate. Yes, my sin was hate.

Chapter 4: Stepping in the Labyrinth

Reading that was probably painful for you, dear reader. I'm sorry. But to know how drastically different this new way will be, you have to know how atypical most of my previous life was. Now you have a grasp of life before strange supernatural things began. Before I entered the labyrinth and began this journey. Let's walk.

After I turned fifty and my kids were capable adults, I realized my natural-born woman would have done a much better job nurturing them. I, as a domesticated woman, had surrendered my God-given common sense. I parented according to the religious framework of others', or an inconsistent mix of influences from my mother and my spouse.

I wasn't afraid of hardly anything: nature, weather, animals, or death. Only one thing scared me: people. People who represented God to me. I'd conformed to a domesticated way because I was afraid of displeasing them. I thought if I upset them, they would turn their back on me for good.

During that same season, I found a tiny bible verse that said when David fulfilled his purpose in his generation, he died. That. I wanted that. A discreet defining criteria for when I'd be finished with life.

I began to pray, "God, please restore me to the person I was born to be, the person you intended me to be."

And I began to look and listen for signs of hope. Hope for a solution, or resolution, to my mess. My hope had always come from somewhere just over the horizon. Like a hunter, I began to pay close attention and keeps my ears open,

I determined to weigh all information coming to me to see if it might be someone's opinion, my own presumption, or directly from the source. I determined to only accept statements, written or spoken, that I could attribute to God or Jesus. No opinion, commentary, epistle or letter. Straight from the horse's mouth.

This wasn't closing my mind, it was opening – and I began listening.

Cinder-rebel

This particular Sunday morning, I was sitting toward the back next to my good friend Hannah. She crossed her limber legs campfire style and opened her bible as he began talking.

Chris, our preacher, always delivered intelligent and enlightening lectures. I took notes in the margins of his handouts every time and reviewed his bible verse references later in the week. He told a warm-up joke while the coffee and donut folks found empty chairs. I readied my pad and pen, primed to be taught.

Stepping in

Chris began to describe the role of ambassadors in host nations, but I knew where he was going with this. I'd heard it too many times in too many congregations.

Another sermon about how we should be good examples so people will be drawn to The Church. I had seen, and experienced, the cruelty of countless "good examples" and seen good people badly damaged by self-righteous "good examples".

That's when God stepped in, interrupted my reality, and began a movie in my head. I hadn't moved. My eyes were still on Chris, but his voice changed to mumbling.

The scene that played out in my mind's eye was set up in the main room of a dark castle.

My straight brown hair was chopped off square just below my ears and my dress seemed to be like those of the 12th century. It came down to about halfway between my knees and ankles, a smudged bib apron gathered at my waist. I had a hand-made straw broom in my hands and my bare feet were checking the dirt floor for particles. The room was about 20 feet square and the walls were made of blackened stones measuring about 10 by 16 inches. The only furniture in the room was a cross legged bench about 18 inches high and 3 feet long placed directly in front of the fireplace. My job, as I understood in the moment, was taking care of that constant fire and sweeping the floor.

As I swept, I heard a slow strong knock. The door was made of thick dark vertical planks and braced with horizontal iron straps. Broom still in hand, I pulled the heavy door open. A tall knight in full armor filled the opening, black against an afternoon sun. He tipped his helmet slightly forward, toward short little me, before he spoke.

"The King needs you to come with me. He needs you to wash feet."

My left hand held the black iron latch of the open door, my right hand held the broom. Time suspended as I comprehended his words. My mind was checking with my heart. Though brand new, this sensation seemed familiar. It felt like when I look in the kitchen cabinet where I keep baking supplies to see if the current inventory supports what I intend to bake.

I spoke no words to the knight but carefully placed the broom against the right side of that open door. After giving the whole space a once-over to make sure all my chores were done, I turned and walked over to the bench. I picked up a red kerchief with my things already tied up inside and followed the King's knight out the door. We turned and walked east.

I came back to the sermon just as it ended and we probably sang a song; I don't recall. Hannah rushed away to work her shift at the coffee shop. No one but me knew my world had changed – drastically. A fundamental transformation happened during this video. In public space, yet private.

God interrupted my life with that daydream. That scene proved to me that God knew my most true nature, a willing servant. I had the reputation of being a rebel because I questioned the status quo of some traditions. Because of this simple scene, I quit jumping to comply with every directive from self-proclaimed religious authorities.

The scene also revealed – to me – that my heart is absolutely open to the call of The King. Not fake kings, the One King. My hesitation at the door was only my spirit verifying that this knight was an authentic representative of The King. Once his spiritual credentials were authenticated with the Holy Spirit, I stepped willingly forward.

Stepping in

This weird event began my walk of the labyrinth metaphor. I'm living a routine life, walking a normal path, then encounter an unexpected turn of my mind, and I walk out from the turn with a new insight. A truer reality.

What I realized through this turn:

- I really do want to serve The King, but only the King. My heart will verify the person who claims to represent The King before going along with a recruitment.
- God's Spirit will authorize his true knights.
- I'm not a rebel.
- And the best thing: God cares enough about one little person, me, to enter my life and satisfy a question

Turn toward Tulsa

I woke up at 4:27 a.m. on a Friday morning in March. A voice (I assume was God since I sleep alone) said, "Go take yourself of the (work) calendar and drive south."

It was the end of March but the weather was our usual moderate Missouri. I loved my job as tutor in the community college learning center. It was fun and always challenging. I never tried to get out of work, even on Fridays.

The tutor lab was an open informal space with five desks for full time staff and five round tables for students and tutors to work together. We kept a large paper desk calendar on the counter with handwritten notes about who was working when, appointments, etc. I hadn't checked it the day before, didn't have any plans except to come to work and see if anyone needed help with Geography, Geology, or English Comp. A regular day.

I didn't second guess that directive or engage basic human resistance at all that predawn morning. I made up my mind months ago to be open to however God expressed himself.

I just got up and threw on jeans, shirt, shoes, and jacket, then grabbed the backpack I kept packed for spontaneous sanity trips. My life then seemed to be splitting in two. The actual marriage and the actual spiritual opening up seemed mutually exclusive and it made me crazy. When pressure built beyond my ability to cope, I'd go stay a day or two at a nearby monastery. During this season of the marriage, we didn't sleep in the same room anymore. I paused at the gentle rhythm of snoring behind his shut door and quietly left.

I drove to the campus, unlocked the building, unlocked the office, turned on the lights, walked straight to the calendar, and picked up a pencil. This day's block was blank; no one had scheduled any appointments. We tutors typically discussed calendar alterations with our supervisor before writing it down. Not this time.

My hand wrote: Carol – out all day. I was aware of what I was doing but it was sort of motivated by "other" forces than my own logic. I didn't think about consequences or consider getting permission from anyone; I just wrote the words. I guess I was trusting God who told me to do this would clear things with my supervisor.

The clock had not yet struck 5:00 a.m. and I was on the highway heading south.

Stepping in

About ten miles down the road, I finally connected the date and direction in my mind and spoke aloud, "I guess I'm going to Tulsa."

My family and I had attended the Soul Winning Workshop held at the Oklahoma state fairgrounds a few times before. The first time, my husband and I left the kids with friends and drove nineteen hours from western Nebraska. The weather was sweet and warm compared to the long frigid winter in the panhandle so we slept in our old conversion van. I saw red bud and dogwood trees in bloom for the first time. What a joy.

The sermons in our tiny churches were dutiful and dry. Tulsa lectures were encouraging and exciting. My husband enjoyed getting to sing acapella with people of his denomination and watch people. I took notes to last me the year and perused the nearly 200 vendor and ministry booths. I'd never seen anything like this!

After we moved to Kansas City and I realized it took only five hours to drive there, so it became our family's spring road trip. The boys were preteen and old enough to enjoy the youth group speakers. Preachers from all over the country spoke. I felt up-to-date and not quite so isolated. I even caught up with folks from other places we'd lived.

We stopped going when life got full with kids and church. Our own church leadership suggested to Larry that Tulsa was leaning a bit liberal so he drug his feet when I asked if we could go and eventually he stopped going with us at all, claiming he couldn't get off work.

I stopped in Lamar, Missouri, to see a precious old friend who worked in a funeral home there and use her bathroom. It was still early morning, but she was already in her office and had no funerals scheduled until that afternoon. I told her I was on my way to Tulsa and she responded that their elders had told the congregation not to go to Tulsa this year. Word had it that someone was going to apologize for the Church's condemnation of using pianos for the last hundred years.

Until that moment, I didn't know anything about what subjects might be lectured on. I wouldn't be able to choose specific lectures or speakers even after I got a paper schedule. In 1991, the titles on the printed schedule didn't agree with what the men spoke about. Each lecture I went to essentially described how the Holy Spirit was leading them. The living aspect of the Holy Spirit had been, up to this point, taboo. It assisted the writers of the Bible and went away somewhere.

Back on the highway, I knew enough to ask questions. Why did God wake me up to go to Tulsa? What am I supposed to learn? I remembered the first sessions began at 9:00 in multiple locations; I'll be late to the first one. Which one is the right one? How do I choose without a program? I inhaled and altered my mode of being, accepting the guidance of the Spirit I responded to a couple hours ago. Settling down and driving efficiently onward to the next unknown.

I arrived on the north side of the main fairgrounds building at 9:10 am. Found an empty parking spot three rows out – weird because Fridays are the busiest days. Accepting this as a mini-miracle because attendance approximates eight thousand people who got here at least an hour ago to register.

I silently asked God "where do I go?" and began to walk. I knew there would be two lectures in the main hall and one in the separate building fifty yards behind my car. I walked matter-of-factly into the huge building, not considering my own desires or even tuning in to myself at all. I didn't take time to register with gatekeepers at the door and no one stopped me. I heard a speaker to my right but my

Stepping in

feet went left. I listened to the other speaker, saw the crowd seated and laughing at his introductory anecdote but just kept walking.

Well, I was heading down to the cafeteria. Usually the women and children's ministries were assigned to this smaller space. Typically, I only wanted 'real meat', substantive teaching, so opted for one of the other three areas. I entered the musty cafe through the squeaky door and discretely sat in a cold metal folding chair. Two guys were up front.

One said, "Church leaders have to make some incredibly hard decisions and here is how you need to do it."

This is amazing! What a meaty message!

I leaned forward and snagged a handout from an empty chair, whipped out my pen and took crazy notes for the next 45 minutes. They went long and when I came up the steps into the main pavilion, the next hour's lectures had already started. I walked – again by God's guidance, not my own information or reasoning the rest of the day. I went to every lecture God told me to, took copious notes, bought the cds God told me to.

Oh yeah, the piano apology? I did find myself in that audience. The guy, Rick Atchley, said he had been praying for the whole year prior to his 50th birthday asking God what he could do with the last half of his life that would matter. The Holy Spirit told him, "It's time to take down the wall we've built between our Christian brothers."

I cried. I married into that rule of law and never understood the anger or the logic they followed to maintain that idea….among other rules.

That session continued for an extra hour. Rick extended the microphone to Bob Russell, the guy from the piano-approval clan, and the two of them shared their process of reconciliation. I felt the great risk they took to step publicly into expressing error and asking whole churches to give up their hundred year feud.

What a gift! I bought their books to bring home and share with my congregation. Silly me.

Another gift was making a sweet spiritual connection with a couple women running a booth. Their group intended to plant a new church in the Kansas City area over coming months. I would connect with them again when that happened.

Before I walked into this experience, I felt like I was the only person bothered by nonsensical church dogma. This frustration was so much a part of me, it was like background static.

This experience was a dynamic turning point. God woke me up and told me to do something in the wee hours of the morning – and I obeyed. Simple. I held God's hand and turned. Turned and walked.

Because of that turn, I now know:

I heard God. And I complied with God only; didn't chicken out because of religious leaders' say-so. That open-minded response changed my life. I wonder how many times God attempted communication with me before and I just didn't hear. Maybe too intellectual or self-willed to listen.

God gave me an unexpected and precisely perfect gift that weekend. One that keeps on giving love and mercy.

Stepping in

My Name is Caleb

I always tried to get too many things accomplished Sunday mornings before I leave the house. One more load of clothes in the washer. One more plant watered. And this September morning, one more tomato sliced for my breakfast. Then I rushed off to church.

As I passed the grocery store on my right, I heard a voice. I couldn't tell where it came from. I was alone, didn't have the radio on, just thinking, as usual. The voice said, "Your name is Caleb." It was audible, strong, nondescript, and clear.

My simple response was also out loud. "Cool. That explains a lot." And a following thought, *I'll have to research more about this, what it means and why Caleb.*

I put the incident on hold – like so many other things – and drove a little farther to church,

I backed my beat-up Nissan into a tight spot between an old black Chevy pickup and a green Toyota Camry. Grabbed my book bag and ran up the grassy slope and through the glass double doors of this old school building. The metal doors made it pointless to try to be quiet even though I was already a little late for bible class.

I eased into the small classroom. All the chairs around the long tables were taken. No problem; no table or chair necessary. I just settled onto the floor in a corner, crossed my ankles, and spread my bible to my side. Notebook on lap, pen in hand. Ready to learn.

Chris introduced this new class by first telling us it would be different. His objective was clear.

"We're going to go deeper than may be comfortable to some. Into some challenging personal areas." He warned we'd be pushing the model of faith into real, daily life.

I was so excited to hear that. I had already experienced a few encounters with God's messages by way of dreams and visions, but didn't have a safe group of people to talk about them. I felt hopeful. This body of believers, my family for the last fifteen years, was still a bit legalistic but slowly opening up to this sort of living faith idea.

He addressed concerns and read a few verses that modeled discipleship, but before he released us, Chris gave the week's assignment. He said, "I want you to go home and read the book of Numbers. Then I want you to pray and ask God what your spiritual name is."

Oh, my! I already knew! I heard the words less than an hour ago! God told me, "Your name is Caleb" - clearly – in my car on my way here.

God was telling me something before the question was even asked! How weird. I used to point out little miracles to my kids and call them weird God moments. This was one of those, a weird moment for sure.

I caught up with Chris and walked alongside toward the auditorium where his podium waited. I told him that I already knew my name: it was Caleb. He smiled, kept walking, and said, "We'll talk more about the concept next week."

I can't say I remember the sermon that followed. I was preoccupied with applying my new name and its meaning to various

Stepping in

circumstances of my history. It explained so many of my responses in situations, both work and family. Caleb supported Joshua after they returned from the land God told them they would take. Like Caleb, I really don't like to lead; I prefer to support a strong principled leader. A leader, like the knight, whose mission is authentically God's.

Caleb was a faithful optimist. Twelve leaders of God's people set out to examine a territory. They all knew God had promised the land to them. After that scouting trip though, only Caleb and Joshua trusted the invisible God instead of the visible features. The land of giants intimidated the rest.

People sometimes accused me of ridiculous optimism, but I'd rather trust a weird invisible God than visible, touchable, yet unreliable distractions in front of me.

That next week of class never came. Chris died that Thursday. His wife, Maxine's, cancer had returned and she would begin chemotherapy again. While talking with his adult kids at dinner about their mother, his heart broke and its main artery split.

What an amazing gift he gave me before he left. Thanks Chris. Thank you, God.

It's a curious mystery why God wove my life with Chris' this way. What if I hadn't gone to class that day? I was running late. I could have just gone into the general class and avoided embarrassing myself. Apparently, I needed to step into the situation and learn God's name for me.

That happened years ago; I'm comfortable now with my name and nature. However, I've learned there is a big difference between Caleb and Pollyanna. Pollyanna chooses not to see circumstances as they really are; Caleb sees the real situation but chooses to express her confidence in spiritual criteria.

I discovered new truths through this weird encounter. God speaks outside of linear time. The voice of God sounds normal and is not gendered. And God named me according to my true character.

In Grid We Trust

My daughter met me in Ft. Dodge, Iowa for a girls' play-day. We delighted in each other's company and restocked her holiday craft cabinet, disregarding the biting cold November wind and drab grey skies.

She headed back home to Minnesota and family that afternoon. I settled in the hotel room for another night and planned to enjoy a little retreat before going back to work. I bought Chinese take-out, expecting to hole up for the night, finish reading my current book and make a good start on a bottle of Monterrey Riesling.

Half way through the beef and broccoli, a slight shift of light and shadow enticed me to peek around the curtain's hem. A brilliant blue sky had replaced the heavy grey day.

Like a bullet, I ran down the hall, out of the hotel, and planted my stocking feet in the middle of their west parking lot. Victorious white wisps were dancing all over that fabulous blue sky. With my

Stepping in

outstretched arm, the sun measured two whole fists above the horizon.

Hmmm. Do I withdraw to my warm meal and cozy room? Nope. I have an idea!

I was always up for an adventure, and by golly, I had daylight! Which of the great explorers ate all of his meals hot anyway? This was an excellent time to scout the perimeter of this community, investigate this Iowa hinterland, and check out "the grid."

I loved being a geographer! Geography is a discipline that appeased my continual pursuit of *Why?* And *Why's* reply often uncovered astonishing answers and even more captivating questions. This day's expedition could well answer another haunting question: Can we trust the grid?

In geographic context, the grid, actually named the Public Land Survey System (PLSS), is that graphic scar that remains on our land from surveys initiated in 1785. Thomas Jefferson wanted to lessen any trouble with boundary issues when the Revolutionary War soldiers were paid their promised land, so he proposed this clever rectangular scheme to Congress.

All states except Hawaii, Texas, and the historic thirteen colonies document their landscape according to the Public Land Survey System (PLSS). Even today, landowners demonstrate effective use of arable land by compressing farmsteads into the corners of rectangular sections.

Traditional and zealous geographers, like me, find comfort in this grid during our travels. Roads neatly line the edges of these "quarter of a quarter of a quarter" aliquot parts, adjusting at meridians and baselines.

I compiled a list of geographer questions:

- Why do people choose to live here?
- What drives the local economy?
- How do these folks treat their land and water?
- Why do they make the choices they do?

With tennis shoes barely tied, I grabbed my wallet, keys, and coat and rushed from the room. I left the Iowa road map open on the foot of the bed. I'd been studying every detail since yesterday: highways, rivers, population patterns, railroads.

One last glance and I affirmed, "I won't need a map. This is Iowa. Trust the grid."

Just south of this hotel laid a westbound public road and gypsum company that I was curious about. *If I start there, I'll be able to drive west and drink in this brilliant sun a little longer.* The unpainted asphalt road was narrow and hugged the southern city limits, sharing residential back yards and crisscrossing single railroad tracks.

On the west side of town, Business Route 20 dipped into the steep, deciduous vale of the Des Moines River. This terrain feature could prove a serious snag in my plan to trust the grid. I needed to keep in mind that state and local governments can only afford a limited number of bridges, so a local road could reasonably stop short of crossing any substantial stream.

This Des Moines River is bold and determined, full-bodied but not bloated or sluggish. If she were on a menu with the Mississippi, the Big Muddy would be a buffet table, the Des Moines would be a succulent prime rib dinner. Its young age showed by its angular cut

Stepping in

into the otherwise flat land in this region and I wondered what sources fed its tributaries.

Some of the hardwood trees were still vivid yellow and red along the river's ridge with some core leaves still green down in the basin. On the ascending slope, small white words on a coffee-colored sign said this was the Dragoon Route – an 1830's cavalry group that noted the topography of the Des Moines River. I backed off the gas pedal so I could jot notes for later investigation of this new curiosity. I added to my list of questions: What is a Dragoon? Why 1830?

West of Fort Dodge, U. S. highways 20 (east and west) and 169 (north and south) intersected. They seemed to ignore township section lines as they ramble through adjoining states. Moving out of the city's grid system, a petite brown sign invited me to turn north onto Highway 169 toward the next town, Humboldt. A town named Humboldt? This is a good omen for geographers. The grid surely must be trustworthy here. Except for Napoleon Bonaparte, Alexander von Humboldt was the most famous guy in Europe at the turn of the nineteenth century. He studied the natural sciences before we split them into specialties, and particularly, he was the leading personality in physical geography.

Five miles farther, I considered turning east on the road to the airport but I hadn't seen a wind power generator yet. One of the notions that I hoped to confirm was that the incessant wind on this tabletop terrain provides a perfect location for them. (At the time of this publish date the area is densely populated with wind generators.)

Turn right at Badger? No, it would be too easy to head back now. The sunset to my left had been fantastic and was still too precious to drive away from. And I'd added an objective of driving to the town named after von Humbolt.

Dusk turned to dark about five minutes after the sun disappeared. Only a few pink cobwebs were left hanging high in the sky. *Trust the grid. I'll be able to find home base when I get ready to.*

Have I already said Iowa is flat here? I should have been able to spot Humboldt town up ahead even against the quickly dimming horizon, but all I saw was a smattering of farm lights. Even now darker, I was committed. Again, the internal chant: *This is Iowa. Trust the grid.*

"Aha! Trees ahead! Of course!"

I remembered – from the map on the bed in room 24 – that Humboldt was situated near the confluence of the east and west forks of the Des Moines River. This must be it. In the pitch dark, I leaned right (even behind the steering wheel) and descended toward the river and what I hoped was the center of town. Climbing the opposite bank, an avenue of peach-tinted street lights stood at attention, perfect in each place as if surveyed by the sunrise on a mid-June morning. My face beamed while my nervous, unsteady mind sighed that peaceful proverb: *Trust the grid.*

I expected this adventure had peaked and I'd gone about as far away from Camp Super 8 as I wanted to this day. I tried to calculate where I might actually be according to the road map. That map. The one relaxing at the soft warm foot of my costly queen mattress. Exactly how far east or west of straight north of Ft Dodge might I be? The most direct route southward without interruption is the way I just traveled. But what about The Grid? The adventure?

I determine to carry out this experiment. Now, which of these perpendicular trails would present a sure path back? I'd need to tap into my inherent hunter's mindset.

Stepping in

A half-moon was now visible beside the rear view mirror, confirming that I was proceeding generally eastbound but that still didn't tell me about roads. Might they be through roads or interrupted?

The present road was paved and had a faded centerline. That's a pretty good indication of importance. It was deep, dark night now and no visible traffic lights indicated any dominant route. Following the pavement, I turned right, left, then right again and stop at the T intersection. I turn left onto C58, and assumed I was driving east. I wished I was more familiar with road-naming conventions used by the Iowa department of Transportation (DOT). Does the "C" mean County?

The Grid was evident here but not understandable to me. Driving two measured miles seemed to take ten minutes. I was a tiny bit uncomfortable and irritated. Maybe scared. I turned southbound and at a quarter of a mile, I ran into gravel. A pickup met me with its headlights on high beam, which meant that oncoming traffic (like me) was unexpected.

A tiny bit more scared, I turned around. At the next stop sign, I turn right, back onto pavement, and met a two-vehicle caravan coming from, I hope, somewhere populated. Behind them, I saw a fifty-five mile per hour speed limit sign. A very positive indicator.

A few minutes at 55, another stop sign, and another right turn. This time on to a wide paved road painted with a newly painted centerline. A speeding pickup quickly overtook me. Its fresh wash lead me to think the driver might be headed to town on this Saturday night.

Fort Dodge came out from hiding below the curvature of the earth and I could finally see its lighted form. One last right turn at the PraxAir plant and I nearly skidded the last seven miles straight west into town.

Back in Room 24, I ate cold beef and broccoli and drank warm Riesling. Cozy, warm, and geographically satiated, I reviewed the facts and confirmed my quest. Knowing in truth and experience I can *trust the grid*!

What I know now, what I found to be true:

I tried hard to memorize the map. As I explored, I tried to recall all the details marked so clearly on the map. But there were too many details, too many options. My best efforts failed me as the stress of darkness became a factor. I was scared I would be lost.

But the land survey system was straightforward. In the end, I proved I could trust the principles of that simple grid system to explore and get back home, even without depending on intricate details of the map.

This experience paralleled my realization of how the bible works for me. I can memorize its details and trust its straightforward principles to explore life, but no matter how many specific verses I memorize, scripture is not life. The map is not the territory; the bible is not God!

Chapter 5: Rough Trail

Coward or Courageous

Over the last few months, I'd transitioned from the legalistic congregation who felt like family to the more culturally relevant bunch newly planted by a Chicago megachurch. Life issues common to ordinary persons were the theme of Sunday morning sermons. Contemporary Christian music encouraged my compassionate heart. Particular religious topics along with individual spiritual development were addressed in small groups outside of Sunday morning. I became acquainted with a few other people facing difficult circumstances of middle years.

All of the people in this church home group were divorced – except me. This night, Ed, the leader of the group, made a few references to that, not intending to hurt, I'm sure. He said things like "most of us in here know what it's like to feel rejected because of our divorce."

What the heck does that mean? That someone still in a marriage – like me! – hasn't felt rejection? I beg to differ! I'll bet I have felt more rejection in this thirty-seven-year crappy marriage than the total of everyone in this room.

The pressure kept building during that hour and a half with a couple more off-handed remarks like that one. In my role as his assistant, I kept up support of the discussion even though my body was about to explode. I clamped down my throat during the closing prayer, then collected the aching muscles of my tense body, and slowly stood as Ed said, "Amen".

Holding back a cry and clenching my notebook and bible, I slipped my sandals on as the others moved toward the kitchen for the usual chips, dips, fruit, drinks, and chatter. With a polite "I need to head out" and "I need to go," I slipped out the door. The questioning faces of a couple women indicated they noticed my weak, pinched voice. I tried to hold the cry until I could get into my car and close the door, but halfway across the street, my head tipped back, I found the stars and yelled,

"Am I in this marriage because I'm brave – or because I'm a coward?"

As soon as I could control my shaking, I drove home. Tears blended street lights and headlights on this familiar route. I didn't answer the two phone calls; I had another question to answer.

"If I could do one thing different, what would it be?"

"I would have divorced him in 1998."

Neither of these two thoughts had ever come to my mind before. Fifty-seven years old. Why not? Why now God? Am I somehow more prepared to deal with consequences of whatever comes from stirring this pot?

The next day, I walked into a flat-fee, no-fault lawyer's office and talked divorce options and details for the very first time. After an hour and a half, I felt hopeful and clean, not dirty and evil. I had never considered divorce as an option before. He did not beat me nor did he have an affair, so I understood the marriage contract sticks.

I didn't join this divorce care group because I was in a divorce or even considering the action. I was only trying to get some coping mechanisms and some understanding about how to live with the realities of aloneness? Or the rejection of it all.

One thing I realized was the people who were divorced were not dealing with rejection. In Divorce Care, people were concerned with identifying one's self as an individual now that they were no longer coupled. Discovering their individual identity as a means to deal with loneliness. I still didn't fit. I'd always been alone, and most lonely within the marriage.

No one could know the pain of living with him. Outsiders will believe what they want. My gut was wrenched. My heart broken, again. How do I ask God into this mess?

Before these recent encounters with Spirit, the only way I saw out of marriage was death. Any investigation would show no physical evidence of harm or betrayal. And since the only arms I wanted to run to were God's, then to depart this dimension seemed a reasonable option. Also, to leave my kids now that they're grown would be better. To eliminate me from their young families' lives will let them paint my image to fit their own needs. People will do that anyway.

Nothing looked different on the outside, but I knew inside I'd turned a corner. Whichever answer it was: whether I'd been courageous or a coward, the marriage was now clearly unsalvageable.

What was next? I'd have to have the conversation. First with the kids, individually if possible, then him, but not today. I was learning, finally in my fifties, to play my cards close to my chest. Not because I want to protect myself against other people, but to limit my out-loud processing to a minimum until God and me, together, can work more on the issue – and we have a lot of work to do.

Wizards, Crickets, and Burlap

What I know now is that I'd been believing in all the wrong wizards, like Dorothy in The Wizard of Oz. I'd been trying to conform to authorities that I'd made my wizards. I did that out of love, and believing love is a reciprocal feeling, that they might love me back.

My first wizard was my mother. She raised me on slogans, not conversations. Do as I say, not as I do. It's not where you go but what you do there. What's wrong is those slogans gave me no understanding or context by which to develop my own reasoning. Don't ask questions, just try harder.

The second wizard was my husband. I learned biblical slogans, verses plucked from their context to fill his quiver. I learned gender roles, but, when he delegated his to me, they were mine too. No questions answered. No reasoning or discussion allowed. Do my duty and don't be more trouble than I'm worth. What was wrong with this is that we lived a nice life but never grew to be a couple. He owned me from 1973 on and he declared my value.

Another wizard I chose was church leadership, to be more precise, religious bullies. I learned I would not go to heaven unless I had children and saw to it they went to heaven. Yes, that was taught in multiple congregations in multiple states within this denomination. A denomination that claimed each congregation was autonomous. I learned bible lessons by fill-in-the-blank sheets of isolated verses, compiled in order to support a premise. I learned not to talk about God or Jesus, but to maintain the purity of the Church, and abstain from musical instruments or go to hell. The wrongs in this scenario are too numerous to explain.

The basic issue with all these wizards is that I chose each one. Discovering much later they could never be more than a miniscule portion of the greatest wizard, I AM. I had not heard of God, church, or Jesus until I met my husband at age twenty, but naturally sought that sort of higher power outside myself. And when introduced to religion, I grabbed desperately at anyone who seemed to know about God.

I'd been trying as hard as I knew how. My attempts to do better were sincere, studying to learn more about God, but all tangent to the real thing. I was done and no better off than before.

Stepping deeper

I had read that John of the bible lived weird because he totally committed to his purpose. He ate wild honey and locust and wore camel hair as part of his resolve. I was desperately miserable, fed up with living, and now totally committed to this strange pursuit. I'd worn burlap and eaten beans as a kid on the farm.

At the moment I realized the parallel, I swore aloud, "God, I'll eat crickets and wear burlap for you. I just want to know you!"

I'd been taught in the church that to swear an oath is a sin, but this didn't feel like a sin. It felt like I gave my word, shook hands on a deal that asserted my commitment. I didn't think about consequences, didn't care what happened next. I took my first deliberate steps into the unknown. I couldn't put accurate words to it yet, but I had just begun hunting the real God.

PART TWO: WAYFINDING

Chapter 6: Walk or Wait

What now?

What happens now? Do I wait? Ask more questions? Read more books? Where do I read? What do I do? What's the most right thing to do?

I remembered the motivational speech I gave at the Emotions Anonymous convention in Chicago in the early 1990s. While I spoke, I also prepared a huge dill pickle for an experiment on stage. I set a table lamp on the podium and cut the cord from it off and stripped back the latex covering, leaving raw wire ends. I twisted them firm and poked them into each end of my pickle. I set the unsuspecting pickle across a styrofoam cup and asked the audience if they believed the Twelve Steps worked.

Walk or Wait

I compared that wired pickle to our homes. "Our home may have electricity hooked up and turned on, but if we never flip a light switch, we'll still be in the dark. If we don't work the Twelve Steps, they won't work. If I don't plug in this pickle, we'll never know if it really will light up like a lamp.

Then I did it. And the pickle glowed – and smoked a little.

That point I made over ten years before related to my faith this day. It was time to plug in my personal pickle of faith. I needed to verify my current belief wiring, particularly after recent audible encounters. Then, engage these new beliefs and see if my faith would light up. Did I completely believe? Or did I just practice rhetorical questioning?

I now knew I could trust biblical principles like I trusted the land survey grid in Iowa. Now I had to prove that by stepping in to that new belief in trust – is that true?

What if bad things happen? How do I know when I mess up?

Over the last few months, undeniable "weird God" events had inserted into my private world. I've drawn some conclusions about God's character from these important encounters. God's spiritual behaviors had been precise and helpful, so I agreed to cooperate with whatever God had in mind. I had to surrender to trust – and wait for as long as it took.

Like a radio dial, I tuned my mind and heart to look more deliberately for the invisible – to listen for the voice of the Shepherd.

The shepherd idea came from the book of John in the bible. I never got comfortable calling God God; it seemed like saying, "Hey you." It seemed okay for me to be called, "Hey Teacher" in the classroom but I thought I could do better regarding God.

Chapter ten offered the metaphor of God as a shepherd. Actually, The Great Shepherd and he knew his sheep by name. He already proved he knew my name. He noticed me even though I was an old ewe with bits of trash from the pen stuck in my wool. He saw my scars of living (mostly covered) and knew each scar's story. Scars from stupid sheep keepers and from my own bumping up against the barbed wire of the pen.

When I read John 10, I chose to accept it as true. No one ever really called me by my name. Mom called me by a combination of mine and my baby sister's name Kelley: Caroley. My husband called me wife, even when we moved to a new church. "This is my wife." The kids called me Mom.

Not only does the Great Shepherd call each sheep by name, but calls them out of the sheep pen into good pasture. This was my sweetest hope. I felt like I could amble through the opened gate and munch clean brilliant grass. Lay down in it if I felt like laying down. He said he'd care for the sheep who followed him out to pasture.

I knew He had already called me by my name, and I heard the Shepherd's voice that day.

When my son sang in a large college choir, I could hear his unique voice. I recognized it out of the mass of voices. He's my son. When I hear birds in the woods, I recognize the voices of the hawks, cardinals, junco, and grosbeak because I've worked at listening. I've watched musicians jam and am always overjoyed when I see the ears of a veteran pull closer to the new player. And watch the new player move closer to who he's playing with. A musician's ears are their greatest tool.

So, at this desperately critical time, my main concern would be listening. It was my character to fix things, to take action, but I'd surrendered this fixing to the Great Shepherd, God, for an unknown time. My work was to lean in and learn to recognize the voice of the Great Shepherd.

Wayfinding

So, I was on an adventure, a journey. A journey to no specific destination except to get to know the authentic deity that created this incredible universe. I'd witnessed the natural world close up since I was a baby. As a kid, there was no power greater than Mom, but as an adult, I'd settled on God being the coordinating intelligent entity behind all those wonders. Marrying into church and legalism killed or starved any child-like wonder about who or what this entity might be.

The wonder was back, with an edge of tension. The few encounters, audibles, visions, and lucid dreams that occurred over recent months intrigued me. I'd experienced a personality caring enough to connect with me without ceremony and direct enough to disrupt my errant thinking. I hoped the truth of that deity would be just over the next hill. What might I find?

This territory was all new to me – this chaos of a family coming apart. Waypoints unmarked. No map of routes to follow. However, I understood wayfinding was not the same as being lost. Neither was wayfinding the same as religious wandering. I wasn't lost and I wasn't wandering aimless. Maybe I was off track. I'd walked years thinking one way, maybe a wrong way, maybe right. Either way, I was ready for God to take me by the shoulders and turn me, and point out the things I should be looking at. Like a parent might turn a child, point to a bird that was in the tree all along, so the child finally sees the bird.

I set aside the church teachings like I set aside the map in Iowa. Fundamental traditions had been passed down by too many biased individuals and had proved unreliable compared to the Shepherd. I was searching for the truer way of God. For this purpose, I removed the road signs and pavement of fundamental religion. I just wanted to clearly grasp how unconnected things of this world might connect in God's world, not limited by time, chronology, or physically sensible effects humans depend on.

I grew up in expansive open skies and pastures where roads weren't important. I knew specific features of the thousand acres of our home place terrain but didn't use roads to get from one to another. The events, experiences of this journey were like landscape features with no roads to connect them. I encountered the weird and witnessed undeniably God things that turned my mindset 180 degrees.

What I now know to be true is I'd go through some staggering hard times and gain astounding insight, but not see any of it coming. Spiritual encounters and traumatic emotional experiences were like waypoints I had to pass through. The Shepherd, God, had introduced himself as an unseen voice inside and outside my head. My challenge would be to trust an invisible God or fall back on my own strength and archaic religious patterns of thinking.

The toughest trial of my life, however, was to grapple with the crazy dichotomy of living through a crappy marriage and growing deep into God at the same time. God pressed me to integrate the two. Horrible injustice one moment and glorious hope the next. How do I make sense of such extreme ugliness and God?

From January through April, vivid scenes of our marriage history presented in my mind's eye like trailers for movies. Random times of day and night. Unsolicited. Stored behind the curtain of my coping mechanisms for decades. Sights, smells, physical sensations popped into the present as if current. I shook my head and tried to

Walk or Wait

throw them out but they persisted. I talked to God about them and He said, "Forgive."

Crap. Now? Why now? How can I?

I didn't doubt what God said but didn't know how to do it. I remembered the threatening order of operations taught in church: unless I forgive, I will not be forgiven. I wanted to please God, but that would be too hard. I tried and tried. God, my Shepherd waited. He let me wrestle with my own options for weeks, then caught me in a receptive state of mind and showed me a holograph-type scene that, in less than a minute, fixed my comprehension of the word and changed me into the status of "forgiving."

I'm standing and swaying to the rhythm of silence. Something draws my eyes to my left and I see a five feet five inch tall lighthouse standing there dark and dormant. I think it's me; more reasonable, a metaphor for me. A beam of light the diameter of a softball comes down from above and pours into the lighthouse. Then the truth of forgiveness happens. The little lighthouse is porous! She is full of holes and the light that's flowing into her flows right out through all those holes – in all directions. There's nothing she can do to stop the flow of forgiving light. In fact, that doesn't even cross her mind. She receives forgiving light from above and forgiving light radiates out of her.

Totally backwards of my archaic religious history. In this moment, that teaching was completely overwritten. This important turning point was also a waypoint early on the journey.

In that event, that turn, I discovered forgiveness is a condition. I am forgiving as a result of receiving forgiving energy from God. Forgiveness moves through me. I don't try to plug holes – withhold – or direct it toward one person. I also make sure my receiver mind is open.

I didn't know then, but I had constant allies along my route, some visible, most not. Science has always been a friend to me. Physics explains functions and behavior in a way I can understand. Algebra formulas explain the functions of a rollercoaster. Kirlian photography captures invisible energy shapes of leaves not yet unfurled.

This is one way I accepted the reality of invisible.

Flatland and Sphere

Several years ago I came across a book called *Flatland: A Romance of Many Dimensions*, written by Edwin Abbott, a school teacher, published in 1884. The main idea I came away with is that folks that live in a two-dimensional reality have no experiential way to understand additional dimensions. Similar to how we, as simple humans, have no way of understanding unseen things or dimensions of spiritual material.

I'd had the book deep in my collection of more than three hundred books for years but didn't ever read it. Until that winter. I carried it to work and skimmed it over breaks between students I tutored.

That scenario helped me grasp the possibility of dimensions that can't be seen of touched. How to accept the concept of heaven or another dimension that intersects with this physical one.

Walk or Wait

A character, Square, lives in a two-dimensional world, Flatland. His cohorts are other geometric figures. Their hierarchic class is indicated by how complex their shape is, even though they're all still 2-dimensional.

One "day," Square has a dream where he visits a one-dimensional world, Lineland. He tries to communicate with one of its Points, to no avail. The Point can't sense the presence of Square.

Another day, Square is visited by a three-dimensional Sphere, which he cannot comprehend.

Sphere visits Flatland every once in a while in an attempt to introduce one of the shapes to the idea of a third dimension.

Sphere sees the leaders of Flatland secretly acknowledging the existence of the sphere, but also sees them silence anyone found preaching the truth of the third dimension.

After Square's mind is opened to the Sphere, the work of accepting the theoretical possibility of the existence of a fourth (and more) spatial dimension begins. The book's message described social class issues, but I couldn't help but apply it to spiritual issues and noticed some important parallels.

That book provided a logical framework to understand biblical verses about God and heaven and time. Scriptures that point out our human relationship with time and how that restricting force is not part of the heaven dimension. For example, Peter said a day is like a thousand years and a thousand years is like a day. No absolute measure of time. Different rules apply in different dimensions.

Like time, other laws of physics may be adjustable. I heard a preacher use the law of aerodynamics as a simile to the law of grace. The law of gravity is a scientific truth, but the law of aerodynamics is also scientific truth. It is the law of aerodynamics that keeps of an airplane in the air and overcomes the law of gravity. Romans chapter 8 puts it out there: the law of the Spirit of life in Christ Jesus sets us free from the law of death.

I love science, and I hadn't seen good science disagree with scripture. Scripture, to clarify, is not the King James Version of the Bible. So many scholars have studied scrolls, cross-referenced other inspired scriptures, and applied analytical tools of the profession, I cannot base my faith on a collection of books compiled by a committee of men living in the political environment of the 1600s.

I didn't see any reason to separate science and scripture anywhere along this trek of living or look for them to be at odds with each other. If I believed in an all-encompassing God who created everything, then I logically believe science agrees with that.

But could I accept new information, tangible or intangible, and adapt my entrenched responses according to obscure laws and trust new logic outcomes? Maybe – with pickle faith.

This book gave me permission to believe outside traditional ideas about God. I changed from cooperating compliantly with religions' identity markers for God to applying hunting principles. Looking for tracks of God like a hunter would. Like one of the folks in Flatland who looks for evidence of Sphere.

Choking on Church

Fed up. I was fed up with the mishandling – mis-hammering – of bible verses. All the conversations that focused on women being silent and not braiding their hair. What's the value in that conversation in this era? Curiosity or intimidation?

And the "not permitted to teach" verse? In most of the congregations I've been part of, the men would not teach, or delegated women to do it, maintaining their power and authority. Trash. Wimpy trash.

I was fed up with scripture being deliberately misused. In the King James version, Timothy says "study" to show yourselves approved. The principle of the verse was not to study but to earnestly try to live right, to make an effort to apply God's principles in living.

The way it was taught was that we earn God's approval by studying. Thus, Sunday morning, Sunday night, and Wednesday night, church people gathered to "study." I became suspicious that the approval sought was not God's but other members who also liked to speak King James' language?

I'd tried hard to read the bible and study bible lessons. For decades, I'd spread out notes, bible, and reference books on the dining table in the afternoons. I wanted to learn.

I've taught college classes and built tests. I chose which points to test on. Which principles that I think students will need to build on next semester, or will be needed in their employment. I use fill in the blank or matching terms to definitions, typing the definition and letting them select from a list of terms. That's pretty easy but there are usually a couple that are similar enough to be mistaken for each other except for one key element. If they miss that, I know what I need to clarify.

But those kind of test questions don't tell me if a student understands. If I need to evaluate students' understanding of a core idea or a relationship between concepts, I'll build an essay question. Answers, well-written or not, give me insight into their understanding.

Of all the bible studies I've seen, never have I seen opportunity to check for understanding. No space for an essay response. Just fill in the blanks and get on with the doctrine. I saved them all, marginal notes and relevant scriptures for some imagined day when I might have the time to go through each one and line up the steps to understand and agree. Never quite got the time.

Bible study material common in my 30s and 40s shaped my religion. The lessons typically put forward a specific theme by compiled single verse bullet points. Single word blanks for me to fill in made sure I got their **bold** point. This same method of fill-in-the-blank learning was used in avionics school in the military. It was called "programmed instruction."

Here's one I saved. Its theme is not printed. No title, none needed.

Seek God – *pray, fast, read.*
Self-denial – *in God's service*
Submit – *to employer*
Serve – *those in need*
Suffer – *for His name*
Sacrifice – *for the church*
Share – *my time, talents, treasure*

Walk or Wait

You shall be repaid at the resurrection of the righteous. Luke 14:14
Your wages are great in Heaven. Luke 6:23
Must believe God is a rewarder. Hebrews 11:6

Was this really a bible study? Three single verses gathered and typed on paper to sum up this self-righteous agenda?

On the other hand, these "lessons" raised questions for me. Some of the most interesting ideas laid between or next to the verse with the blank. Stuff like grace, mercy, spirit. Ideas that took seed in my curious mind.

It's reasonable to think all this bible study would help me live life better. It didn't. How long had I been doing this? Trying so hard and my life was still a painful mess. I could march to the beat of their bullet points and appear to be in line with Christian behavior, but be dying or dead inside. I couldn't stand the clashing of my exterior and interior life.

Bible verses out of context offered me bite after petty bite but I could not swallow anymore. I got reprimanded countless times for asking deep questions. Questions about context, or terminology.

"If wives are to submit themselves to husbands in this verse, why do we skip over the next verse that talks about husbands loving wives?"

"This section refers to the Holy Spirit. How does that fit with this answer?"

Things became intolerable. I didn't quit, I just choked.

I was growing more and more aggravated. Probably from seeing too much cover-up from inside the church. I saw too many situations, regular human situations, which were mishandled by leaders in order to preserve the appearance of having a pure church. Claiming to follow the letter of the law (meaning Bible) yet avoiding any mention of any spiritual aspect.

For instance, my husband and I were called over to a couple's house one Saturday night. They'd been married ten years and had three little kids. The husband had beaten his wife and shot a rifle off toward the ceiling. The kids were crouched in one of the bedrooms. He agreed to go somewhere else for the night.

The very next morning, Sunday, that abusive jerk was given permission by church leaders to stand at the podium in front of almost two hundred people and beg his wife to let him come home. Cheri, with bruises covered by her jacket, and the kids sat together in a pew in the middle of the congregation during his performance.

She never expected him to be at church. I didn't expect him to get the attention of the whole church and blame her for rejecting him. That man never said a thing about his own actions that night or previous incidents. He got the microphone because he was a man and had a suit jacket on.

Cheri reported the incident to the police after church services and got a restraining order. Two of the church elders made a visit to her home later that week and suggested family counselling. Why didn't the elders, six of them, deal with this better? That same Sunday evening, I asked.

"How did you guys decide to let him get up front with the mic? Did you consider how Cheri and the kids would feel? This isn't the first time he's done this. I've told you about their situation before. Where did that fit in your meeting this morning?"

They just shrugged.

The church had a structure in place. It was operating from unwritten traditions that held more power than the written scripture people claimed to go by. I don't even know where prayer fit in. They didn't mention it.

Questions.

Why? Two institutions set up by God: church and family were the two causing the most pain.

Where would I get answers? That one book, the bible? I had a problem with that idea. A selective crew of men hundreds of years ago decided which documents to include in the compilation that millions now count as singly valid. I couldn't choke that down.

I determined to gather information about God and spiritual subjects from books that didn't make the cut by that crew of ancient men. I dug into catalogs of my favorite two library consortiums, one included the library of religious colleges and monasteries. I determined, however, not to be a devotee of any particular author. A bunch of books affected my journey, but only sections of them and only as they made a solid connection or turn my face to see a thing new. Books were important allies as I turned from fundamentalism.

Chapter 7: Who's with Me?

Hawks from God

I peeked at the faint sky out my bedroom window this fall morning and determined it was near dawn, guessed it between 6:00 and 6:30. Instead of stumbling down the hall to the kitchen for coffee and a clock check, I stayed in bed, wide awake, listening for God. Eyes closed, I asked God what he wanted to say to me and heard, "better choices".

A minute later, I peeled out of warm flannel sheets, slipped on heavy socks, shuffled to the room next door, and slid into the office chair at my desk. Pen in hand, I scooted up to my writing pad to stare out the window.

Just then, two hawks crossed right in front of me! One flew south to north, the other flew north to south slightly higher and neither one more than ten feet away. I gasped and blinked hard.

Where did they go? I couldn't see where they went. Seconds later, they swooped by me from the opposite direction, wingtips nearly touching, one flying a little lower than the other and banking in a slight turn. Like a Blue Angels air show.

Who's with Me?

At that moment, I knew God was talking! I leaned forward and froze. My eyes darting toward every leaf quake, every slight motion, looking for more. Then, I don't know how, but those two huge birds swooped upward from somewhere below the window. Side by side, up and over the roof above. Their white bellies and underwings incredibly close to my face.

When, in life, have I ever absolutely known I was in THE right place at THE right time? This moment, I knew. I didn't leave that position for over two hours. I could not.

This was undeniably a message from God, using his creation, animals I respected. I stayed at the window for a long time after, alert to the possibility of more. I wanted to extend this "better choice" as long as possible.

This event was affirming that I had made a better choice: to write prayer here rather than drink coffee in front of my morning farm show. I have such a distractible mind that I am sure I would have forgotten the words he gave me just before I left my sheets a short while ago. In the moment, I thought the phrase, better choices, was intended for a close friend I was concerned about. We'd been having conversations about his poor choices over the last couple days. True, we can all make better choices, but this morning, I understood that statement applied specifically to me.

As the sun rose, it seemed to light the branches of the trees before the leaves. The hawks seemed to glow, perched on a sun-lit poplar branch, the fourth large branch from the ground. One sat facing the sunrise, the other with his back to the sun, looking left, then right, not down. Regal.

Then I spotted two more sunning themselves and preening on the upper branches of a neighboring tree. This tree had no lower branches; but an eight-foot long broken stub pointing northwest about twenty-five feet up a straight trunk. One hawk there was tugging at pieces of squirrel using his muscles between his shoulders. When he tore a chunk loose, he tossed it to the back of his mouth. This work was delicate, not gluttonous.

About fifteen feet farther up, near the bend of a dead branch, two more hawks perched. One had the features of a younger bird and sat a foot away from its more mature looking parent. Her beak was darker and more curved, arched. Legs and feet a bit deeper orange color. She was sleek, her movements more graceful. The younger, fluffier bird seemed to be pulling out some of his down as he cleaned off damp feathers from his chest and belly.

I looked up from my pages again and saw the two youngsters hopping on the ground. Mom, or dad, was fifty feet up watching the kids bicker, tease, and learn to share – or not. Maybe ownership in hawk society corresponds with the lesson of the Little Red Hen: if you didn't capture the squirrel, you have no part in its consumption.

I wondered if these two were the surviving fledges from the nest attack I watched a few weeks ago. Their ruckus woke me up. I thought they were losing the battle. Raccoons had teamed up to raid the hawks' nest. Those gutsy parents fought off and knocked to the ground three raccoons in predawn shadows. And this day, I saw the beauty of the parents' dedication in these young hawks' survival.

I just couldn't move from that fascinating scene. I prayed a silent prayer. *Thank you, God, for these lives and this lesson. Thank you for nudging me to make this 'better choice'. You know my constant fight to know where I should be and what I should be doing. You show me in this moment. I am grateful.*

Families of hawks built nests high in the trees of my yard nearly every year. The dignity and beauty of their bright breasts in the sunlight

Who's with Me?

was striking. Distinct dark horizontal lines across the end of their abrupt tails identify their group.

Swooping gracefully, they move through the trees like cross-country runners. The way their flight path rises and falls among the hardwood timber, dips, climbs, and corners has that same fluidity as runners over their solid terrain.

I listen for the young ones' voices. Their squeal is not the deep pure scream of mature hawks shouting victory from high, but more pubescent and timid, still unsure of their follow-through.

That hawk event was an important turning point in my learning to notice God, learning to listen.

I walked away from that with new truth. Maybe it should have been obvious to this nature girl before. I acknowledged that God could cause a donkey to speak the language of the man beating him, like the story in the book of Numbers. But now I know he can speak to me through hawks.

I learned hawks were my allies on this journey. A constant reminder and reward for making better choices. And I know they are a gift from God because the writer James said every good and perfect gift is from God.

Hawks usually position themselves about three-fourths of the way up the tree and fairly close to the trunk. Not at the tops of trees or the flimsy edges of branches. When I'm troubled down here, I put my mind in the position of a hawk and look at the situation from that view.

I discovered, and know to be true, that sometimes sitting and staring out a window qualifies as a "better choice."

Stand alone

There's a story in the bible about a married couple named Ananias and Sapphira. They sold a piece of property just to give those proceeds to the apostles. The wife agreed with her husband's idea to keep some back. The money wasn't the problem; the problem was that the husband lied about the amount. Peter called him on it and he dropped dead on the spot. It wasn't about the money, it was about Ananias' integrity. God knew the whole picture.

Three hours later, wife Sapphira answered Peter's question with the agreed upon lie. She dropped dead – same spot.

I'd probably read that before, but this time, I realized I could step out of the role of being my husband's "yes man". If agreeing with him goes against my own integrity, I don't have to. Each of them was individually accountable. My cognitive dissonance was resolved though I had no idea how my new decision might play out.

The religious system was fixed to make sure he was always over me. After five years in the military, I understood rank. I knew I was supposed to endorse the spouse even when I knew he was being lazy, unspiritual, and fudging the truth.

But right then, I decided that since I'm individually accountable to God, I'll make the choice to drop dead because of my own lies. I would not cover his anymore.

Who's with Me?

An old saying states: If you can't say anything good about someone, don't say anything at all. A long-time friend, Karen, actually never spoke negative about anyone. I recognized how she felt when she clammed up in a casual conversation. I respected her strength and grace. This would be my strategy.

I know now that choices, bad ones or better ones, are singly mine.

Scout

Driving the Iowa interstate northbound on my way to Mom's for the weekend. Only a day after a March blizzard, the main roadways had been mostly cleared. Across the median, I saw the rear half of a vehicle that had plunged deep into the windblown drift and a barbed wire fence.

In a split second, my face contorted in a silent, tearful cry of intense longing. That scene opened an emotional funnel straight into my soul. It wasn't the cold deep snow drift, nor the vehicle. I had never been inspired by tundra images or boats breaking ice in the frozen northern rivers and seas.

Surprised by my reaction, I tried to figure out why this scene would make me cry. My mind showed me the physical composition of my world, my own life. Square-cornered furniture, appliances, and walls. Round flowerpots and cups. Every space composed of things already touched, controlled, or manipulated by man.

But this blizzard created a virgin environment: the severe angle of these drifts, the overall depth of the snowfall, and the forward movement of that car breaking that drift. In that situation, I felt emotions of an explorer again – and I missed it terribly! The adventure of being on the front edge of something yet undiscovered!

On the plains and pastures of my young time, I enjoyed that sense of exploring and even some of the words. "Has any person ever walked *here*? Or *here*?" I think my purpose for each hike was to hunt for that place.

As I topped each treeless hill, I confirmed no person in sight and human structures were a minimum of two miles, better yet, five miles away from me. I felt comfort and peace, then declared it safe enough to explore. Explore each square foot and its relationship to the next geographic level. Like the relationship of Earth and moon, planets and solar system, Milky Way and endless Space.

My sister called me Scout. When I wondered about a thing, I tried to satisfy that wonder. That interest in the beyond.

In my early adult life, my motto was: "Life is an adventure to be lived." On the road, behind the wheel, I could live. No people to influence my head; no mirror to limit or define my identity. No duties. No obligations.

My mid-life label for myself, life-long learner, described the attitude of an adventurer also. Like the snowdrift image, I can't know what lies beneath; the snowy disguise does not necessarily parallel earth's true contours underneath. To solve that mystery, I gather my best logic and harvest previous experiences, then proceed to dig out answers from under the surface.

So, why had I lost this authentic sense of myself now? How had I gotten so boxed in? I wasn't afraid of nature, weather, isolation, God, babies, animals, or death. What was I afraid of? People and loss of freedom. Cramming my spirit and soul into someone else's container worked for a few decades (not well).

After I turned fifty and my kids were adults, I realized my natural born woman would have done a better job nurturing them through their youth. This domesticated mother didn't trust her God-given common sense. I didn't have nurturing in my own history but intense family love motivated me.

I prayed that God restore me to who I was born to be, the person he intended me to be.

Getting to Know You ♪

Another **ally** on my search, this trek toward the unknown real God was the human Jesus as described by the book of John. After three decades of preaching, I was still confused about what the connection between God or Jesus and me was supposed to look like. Who was I supposed to pray to? What if life was so problematic because I wasn't praying to the right entity? I had a lot of information but still no comprehension of a clear definition of a human's access to God.

I decided to shelve material about living the right way; that had not solved the problem. I would reject anything shot toward me as single verses or sections of letters to churches.

I decided to focus on the simple: Jesus' dialog typed in red. I should be able to read and understand straightforward sentences of Jesus. At the same time, I chose to accept as a true fact that Jesus lived on earth as a person who came from God. Basic position I began with: Jesus was a person, and what Jesus said about himself and life was all I needed. Book to read to get to know Jesus: John.

If I want to get to know someone, my first question would not be, "Where you were born?" If I want to get acquainted with my new friend, Julie, I wouldn't focus on where she's from, her genealogy or family tree. I'd meet her at a place we could talk. We would introduce ourselves and maybe mention interests or employment that takes up our days. We would begin our conversation at the point in life we are now, adults.

I got acquainted with the person Jesus at John's place, his book of their time together as adults. It seemed just like I might reveal different aspects of my personality in different rooms of my house to a new friend. This new friend would learn who I am in my kitchen. That I play music in the second bedroom. My kayak and most of my camping gear is stored in the basement storeroom. She'd learn more about me as she moved from place to place in my home.

I learned various aspects of Jesus' personality and character in John's book. I did not read in order, of course. I felt like the stories happened in certain places, and place is not necessarily explored in linear mode.

The first place had been in John's tenth chapter where Jesus revealed that he was the Great Shepherd and knew my name.

He also said he's not the pen. So I continue to listen for the voice of the Great Shepherd.

He fed people – a lot. Near the middle of John, I met him feeding folks. That's what I loved to do, feed people, but on a much smaller scale. If you came to visit me, I'd feed you well. Now-a-days, it would be plant-based, organic, and herbed-up sumptuously from my garden.

As I read this same place in the Message, I got more acquainted with Jesus as the creator of food and source of drinking water. His take on thirst and true thirst along with his function as an unlimited spiritual drinking fountain is in John 4. In John 6, he expanded fish

Who's with Me?

and bread from one boy to feed four to five thousand people, with leftovers.

The kind of food they ate was physical, touchable, chewable, and digestible. He provided food with compassionate kindness, but explained another kind of food that lasts forever. He kept trying to explain the limited and temporary condition of this physical dimension. Forever food satisfies. He said the bread he just created nor the manna bread they knew from Moses's time in the wilderness are as real as bread from God that feeds our spirit. Another weird reality.

Then it gets even weirder when he says that He himself is the real food and drink that keeps people alive. I still don't comprehend this, but whenever I read it, I try to capture the concept. There's a physical person living in a physical dimension and a whole other spiritual person living in essence in an invisible-to-us dimension.

That's what he does, provides food. But later, I learned how disappointed He was when people only wanted to be close to Him because he provided food. I understood that too.

John, the author and friend of Jesus, seemed to think in function more than appearance. I, too, think in function much more than how things appear. When I read a piece that describes part of life as "the appearance" of something, good or bad, I'm uncomfortable. I guess from too many years of holding together the appearance of a good life. I thought that was "putting your best foot forward." Honesty was a high priority to me but I also thought we were supposed to clean up before we go to town or have company over.

However, when I'd give my best answer to someone's question, they would pause, then turn away or change the subject. I thought the function of a question was to pursue an answer to the question.

John uses the word believing 100 times as a functioning verb. Its function is to **be,** not to appear like a good example of a believer, but to functionally believe. And believing is the portal to this abundant pasture life he beckoned his sheep with.

Jesus got angry when some didn't believe. I saw this at his good friend's funeral. He didn't attend Lazarus' funeral to mourn; he came to fix things, to resurrect his friend so people would believe in an incredible God. But I've never seen Jesus so angry and let down as in this place, John chapter 11.

Lazarus and sisters, Martha and Mary, were close friends of Jesus and had no doubt witnessed some amazing miracles during the time they hung out together. They believed in his God-ness. Jesus had confidence in their faith, so when he heard Lazarus was sick, he thought Mary and Martha would trust him to fix the situation.

By the time he arrived, the funeral was going strong. Sympathetic folks from town were gathered in support of the family. The sisters complained to Jesus that he could have prevented death. When he reminded them about people being resurrected and living forever, they thought he was referring to the end of time resurrection.

As I read, in my mind I saw Jesus' face. I saw his eyes looking hard at Mary. Her tears. She felt let down by her good friend. He looked past her at the folks around her. Then, several translations specifically say, anger welled up within him.

In that moment, I understood why Jesus wept. Because he was deeply frustrated and upset. All the years he'd already spent with this population. All the trouble he'd gone to, miracles he'd done, healing folks, so that these people might believe he was the Son of God, that he lived to provide hope for them. And as he looked at them, he realized they didn't believe him.

Who's with Me?

He knew in just a few days he'd be tortured and killed for the sake of these same people God loved. I related to his frustration anger, though my history of being let down pales with his. Farther down in that section, at the tomb, anger wells up in him again because of the mumbling doubters walking along.

Jesus looks up and calls to his Father God. "I know you hear me, you always have, but for the benefit of these people, so they might believe you sent me, I say, 'Lazarus, come out!'" And Lazarus did.

Some people believed, some still didn't. Some reported him to the religious bosses.

Turning point.

I began to wonder how many times in my life I had experienced weird things, strange and miraculous things, and given the credit to coincidence or chance. Good fortune or luck. Or anything but a loving God who Jesus called Father.

We have a saying here in the Midwest: "give credit where credit's due." After my mind saw Jesus' face at this place of the funeral, and his deep frustration and hurt, I decided to give God credit for every good thing in my life.

I now accept as true that whether it's the aspect of God called Holy Spirit, or God's offspring man, Jesus, or angels, or other good spirits, I'll let that be a mystery. But I'll no longer be timid about the source. I don't want to be part of that cause of Jesus' tears. God's system is everlasting lovingkindness and I'm living in that system.

Chapter 8: Praying

Weird – but better

Studying prayer had tied me in performance knots for years. I felt like I always did it wrong. Details were set by classes or books. But by this point in my life, I understood that knowing *about* God was not the same as knowing God. I was ready to experience prayer, not just know *about* prayer. To listen for and learn to recognize the voice of God.

I read a pamphlet about centering prayer, then skimmed a few books by Thomas Keating and Henri Nouwen. The dedication of such people to living and breathing God fascinated me. Sitting quietly for 20-minute sessions challenged me. Warnings of hippy drug cultural history were lost on me. I didn't care who did what then or what movement hijacked this ancient practice. If this discipline is described in scripture and grows me toward God, I'm in.

I chose "Yes Lord" for my mantra and used it to bring my focus back to now and let distractions float by. I read a bit of Gregg Braden who described different modes of prayer across the world. Monks' chanting. Indigenous people sensing water drops on their outstretched palms when they pray for rain.

There is a phrase used in Christian culture that says, "Ask Jesus into your heart." I chose to claim that concept in one of my pre-dawn meditation sessions.

Praying

If Jesus is now with God and the Holy Spirit is alive and with us, then I would open my heart to Jesus in the form of Holy Spirit to clean things up in there and transform my heart environment to what is suitable to God.

I understood that I surrender myself every day anyway, to my own will, to the enemy, or to God. I chose to surrender the work of transforming my heart to God's Holy Spirit. Provide access to God's inhabitation of me. When I calmed my busy brain, I heard words that clarify life. I didn't have to say thee or thou, didn't have to make sense of my thoughts or even speak in complete sentences, or speak at all. The vital thing was – and is – to open access to my spiritual heart and agree to listen to Spirit of God.

Zero-Dark God Time

I woke at 3:18 a.m. that first morning to a silent alarm. Actually it was an invitation like the smell of bacon is an invitation. I slipped into twenty-year-old fleece-lined slippers stained with grease and coffee. Wrapped a flannel shirt over my pajamas and shuffled to the closet.

I'd made a nest yesterday to welcome me whenever I next came to spend time here. A bottle of drinking water, bible, legal sized writing pad, and two pens. Even in pitch dark, I had no trouble locating the brass ginkgo leaf at the end of the pull string of the light fixture inside. 40 Watts of incandescent amber glowed above the hardwood library step stool. One plush pillow for my lap.

Meditation. Nothing was required of me but to be here and be present. I'd practiced centering prayer was a group of three to ten people a few times, read the pamphlet. During the day, a half-day Saturday morning (9-noon) at an old re-purposed convent in Kansas City, Kansas. A bell began silent focus sessions of five, then ten minutes. Another venue offered one-hour sessions with women from a community church that used candles, incense, and a timer.

As kind, gentle as these groups were, I felt a lot of pressure still. Pressure to give a reason why I sit on the floor, why I focus on a tree limb outside a window instead of the suggested object inside. I was afraid that 'whatever' came in the space of the room to speak to others would speak the same thing to me. And I didn't want to hear a buzzer, bell, or gong when time was up.

Who should be guiding this time? It was too difficult for me to dissect my daylight hours and their demands into blocks of time and definitely too difficult for me to focus when every dish in view had to be washed. Every dog bark and every phone ring had to be tended to. Once my day began, it pressed forward without pause.

As an experiment, I asked God to wake me up when He wanted me to get up. This first morning, it was 3:18 a.m. I trusted the 'ask' and rolled out of bed.

My dear old friend, Robbie Sikes, modeled this in the early 1980s. She's the mother of twelve and managed a children's home near McCook Nebraska with her husband Jack. She told me how laundry and food preparation continued after everyone was tucked into bed. Her long workdays stretched into early mornings. She rose early to fix Jack oatmeal before the kids stirred and chores began. She said she prayed about that and believed if two hours of sleep was all she got, then two hours was enough. To this day, Robbie is happy and well at ninety years.

The furnace exhaust and hot water heater vent pipes run up from the basement to the roof through the space just behind this closet.

Praying

My back is always warm against that wall. So in that space – perfect, personal, private space – time was timeless. A pillow on my lap, bible and paper on top, pen in hand, and the ears of my heart attentive. Breathing with God.

No audible words came from me; none were required. And no guilt. My husband's church had taught me prayer was invalid unless aloud. Even though I now believed better, I was still timid, so practiced convincing my spirit of her freedoms. Each time, she savored a fresh removal of decades of suppression.

Mantra. Those teaching the practice of Centering Prayer explained it as one of the tools used. When learning to stay focused on the present, meditating, we might think of thoughts as clouds and let them go. My cloud thoughts were vivid and loud, a barrage of mental chatter. I tried several sounds and words to remove this chatter from these sacred moments of my mind. Some words even turned and became the focus, capturing my mind, drawing it away from God to be a thought itself. Not good.

However, when the phrase "yes lord" came out my mouth, I smiled. I'm not one who'd use the title Lord, but these two words are also the title of one of my favorite church songs. "Yes, Lord, yes…..I will trust you and obey…." No distracting concept here, just a gentle whisper calling my attention back to his face.

Thought: did I feed the dog? "Yes, Lord." Thought gone. Thought: errand to run after this. "Yes, Lord." Not now. Later. Two words not part of my usual language before but now functioned to trigger my easy, sweet surrender to the Great Shepherd. Almighty King whom I gratefully and mysteriously love.

It seems strange to say that I felt a presence when there was no physical sensation of a presence. But like hunger, I wasn't 'hungry' after these predawn sessions in the closet. Whether I hunched in the closet for thirty or ninety minutes (I didn't look at a clock), when I emerged, I'd been fed.

Soul True

Somewhere in one of the Thomas Moore books I'd read, *Care of the Soul*, I got permission to imagine. I was in my mid-fifties and still felt bad about using my imagination, like I should be ashamed of having one. I'd been ridiculed by spouse and family for sharing curious ideas and making strange connections. I began to imagine my soul and began to care for it. This new diet of nutritional spiritual food and exercise started in my closet.

During one of those sessions, I imagined my heart as a habitable place. Nice short prairie grass near a pond. Then I imagined myself sitting on the ground uphill from the earthen dam, knees bent, arms folded around them. Then I asked Jesus to come be with me – if it wouldn't be too much trouble, if he wouldn't mind. He appeared, and sat down beside me on dry crunchy pasture.

That was a brave courageous act on my part. Imagining one image at a time. Not a product of any media or coach, but of my own spirit. And none of the negative consequences I'd feared.

Much, much later, I asked if he would clean up and transform, remodel my heart inside and soften it outside. I really have a strong distaste for asking God for anything for myself, but this was an important time to do that. Since then, I've appealed and acquired the understanding of forgiveness, love, and obedience that same way: by simple asking. I just asked Jesus to put clarity in me. He used visual images to seal each concept solid.

Praying

I hid my pain in clothes closets when my kids were tiny. This was not that. Those terrible tears only increased my shame and guilt. The energy, Spirit, with me here was simple and pure, not loaded and heavy.

Not every closet moment included an epiphany; I didn't look for any guarantees. But I chose to be there. To listen, and offer my heart, mind, and soul. To connect with whichever mode of God blessed me each day: the Holy Spirit, the Word, visions of Jesus, or the voice of Yahweh.

The trust that developed from this practice took some pressure off me. I didn't have to clean up my life before I prayed. God was capable of making his environment clean, if needed. Prayer became inviting, not obligatory.

I know now, and am convinced, that prayer is a condition of openness. An open communication channel. Not one directional, not necessarily call-and-response, and certainly not a sugar-daddy request line.

I know maintaining this open channel would be my primary ally while wayfinding.

Chapter 9: Solo Trek

Couples Communication Class

Idealism and love invited me into this marriage. Hope is what kept me there.

I begged him to go to marriage seminars and enrichment weekends for years, starting when I first heard them offered at church. Surely he'd go to a church function. Maybe we would learn something.

"I'm content. You just need to learn to be content," was his simple response.

Finally, twenty-five years later, and mostly because of pressure from his guy friends at church, he agreed. This one might be different. Couples Communication. Safe enough title. January to March, Thursday nights, eight couples and lead by a familiar counselor to the folks at church.

We were taught specifics of communication styles and at the end of each class, we each took turns practicing the technique. A floor canvas marked like a flower with five petals labeled for Feelings, Thoughts, Wants, Actions, and Data. One person moved to the flower and answered the counselor's questions as he or she moved to each petal.

Solo Trek

For example, I stood in the middle while Gary, the counselor asked questions about a topic I chose to explore.

Our daughter was fifteen and old enough to get her driver's permit. A simple enough topic, but Larry wouldn't discuss it. I hoped to get his thoughts in this exercise.

"What are the facts?"

"How do you feel about her driving?"

"What action can you take?"

Straightforward inquiry, no agenda, easy to respond to - for me.

Larry replied with one phrase no matter which petal he stood on.

"What are the facts?"

"I'm concerned about Leah driving."

"How do you feel about her driving?"

"I'm concerned about it."

"What are you concerned about?"

"I'm concerned about her driving."

Our friends giggled a little, then realizing he really didn't see the difference, tried to draw out of him possible responses.

"Are you worried?"

"No, I'm concerned."

He really did not grasp the difference. I could finally see he wasn't capable of any fuller description or deeper thought. Maybe he didn't even understand that deep thought or feelings might be required. Maybe he wasn't intentionally cold-hearted.

We continued with the class but it didn't get better. This new reality knocked all hope of a good relationship out of the realm of possibility for me. Even though this happened in our twenty-fifth year, it changed nothing about our married life. He still went to work, came home, and watched television. I, however, changed my expectations. I realized I was on my own, and even more lonely. I put my hunger for communication on a back burner. Practiced the logic of the Twelve Step's Serenity Prayer and decided to change what I could and accept what I couldn't. My focus turned to college classes, especially Geoscience, and my job as a library page that paid for them.

I realized and now know I'd been dealing with an invisible handicap for thirty-plus years. I know now why I enjoy deep thoughtful conversations with my wonderful, intelligent kids so much. Even when they were young, I was curious to know what they were thinking. I love hearing them share their reasoning, whether it's new and different or predictable.

Monk Time

To be in the house with continual television, without conversation, with his heavy presence was maddening. I was frantic and agitated most of the time. I needed space to breathe. Some place where I could have peace, external peace anyway. Somewhere quiet to calm my frazzle.

I drove a lot, hunting peace on the road. A bag of snacks and water was all I needed to drive out of town and get some sky.

I found a Benedictine monastery in Atchison, Kansas, nestled on a high cliff just west of the Missouri River. It was only thirty minutes from home and provided rooms to guests for a small price. The brothers welcomed me the best way possible: they went about their business while allowing me to walk the grounds, stay in their guesthouse, and eat silent breakfasts with them. Like my own brothers, I felt their guardian strength, and felt no need to explain my troubles.

The first day I spent there, I brought an Eckert Tolle book, hoping to capture ideas that would lead to internal peace. Stayed up all night and read the whole thing with pen and paper at the ready, ready to write epiphanies and supernatural truths. Got nothing. All night until mid-morning – Nothing. Could not get my overstressed brain to flow with reason.

I guess I was there as a retreat, my brain rested for a while anyway. I didn't need sleep, just rest. I settled on a term for the misery of an illogical relationship: cognitive dissonance. It's described as psychological stress that occurs when a person holds two or more contradictory beliefs, values, ideals. Oh yeah. I felt love and hate at the same time.

From this turn, I discovered these brothers were a safe place for me to run when I couldn't take the craziness. I went there often. Spouse didn't know or care. God did.

Your Maker is your husband

The torment of loneliness began in the early years of the marriage. I thought marriage was supposed to be a sweet deep friendship like no other. I always hoped for intimate conversation. All day I'd look forward to talking with him, learning more about him and his day. But after he ate supper and relaxed with television, he was too tired.

In bed, he would roll away from me. I would wrap my body around his back until his body jerked and I knew he was asleep - about two minutes. Then I'd roll over and cry softly so as not to wake him. Sometimes he just laid flat on his back, eyes shut and hands layered over his chest. Motionless and no interaction. He had to work the next day.

He would be up brushing teeth and shaving at 5:10. I'd stand at the bathroom door and watch. Made fresh coffee but he would get some at work. Out the door by 5:42. No tender morning moments. If I got a goodbye kiss, he watched his wristwatch during the kiss, holding car keys in one hand and briefcase with the other. I hugged him.

How many nights I cried myself to sleep over those thirty-some years.

He now slept in the bedroom down the hall but I could still hear the sweet rhythm of his snoring. Sleeping alone was painful but not as crazy painful as constant rejection. This night, I slept on the green couch – again. Cried myself to sleep – again. Asked God to help me understand what was going on.

In the middle of the night, closer to morning, I sat straight up awake. Not startled but alert. No sounds. Quiet house. Not actively thinking, I stepped around the corner into the dining room and turned on the light. The bible was lying already open on the table. My eyes and heart landed on the upper left section of the page.

"For your Maker is your husband. The LORD Almighty is his name – the Holy One of Israel is your Redeemer; He is called the God of all the earth. The LORD will call you back as if you were a wife deserted and distressed in spirit – a wife who married young, only to be rejected," says your God. (Isaiah 54:5)

I read it over again, and again. I didn't remember ever reading that before, but I hadn't spent a lot of time in Isaiah.

No human could have given me the comfort, consolation, and pinpoint accuracy of heavenly salve to apply to my lacerated heart. That verse attended to my abandonment, feelings of being deserted, and distress of my spirit – all of it. It also made clear that I had – have – a Husband who bought me – paid a ransom – a Redeemer – and that was that. Settled. Hopeful. I would not be abandoned by *this* God-Husband.

I smiled through my sobs. Curled up again on the couch and slept. In the morning, I checked the bible again. Yep, that's what it says. God woke me up with a precious declaration of my status and his relationship to me this season, however long that is. I didn't hunt for that verse. Wouldn't even know what to hunt for. God acted by way of invisible, illogical methods to give me a lifeline. A gift of deep love.

He, the lesser husband, left the first time a few weeks after that. Didn't tell me. Don't know how long he'd been planning to.

God knew. I was not abandoned – am not abandoned by my Maker-husband-Redeemer!

New Mexico Quest

Good morning Kansas.

As Amtrak #3 slowed, Garden City's water tower came into view from my window. A few blocks north of the track and highlighted by sun rays not yet shining on rooftops.

This was the first day of Spring Break and I was on my way to New Mexico to explore the Four Corners region where Arizona, New Mexico, Utah, and Colorado meet. I wanted to find out what the Navajo people believe about heaven. I'd read about how Native Americans pray for rain by imagining and sensing rain. I had questions.

As a geography student, I was particularly fond of a truism that says, The Map is not the Territory. I got this. Maps I produced at school were designed to represent physical features and realistic relationships between them. The intention is to clearly communicate real territory to the user, but maps always came up short. The difference between a map and its territory is the experience.

The map for my spiritual life was the bible; the territory was the actual stepping in to each breath of a situation. And even though a biblical principal may ring true, I just couldn't get a deep level of knowing while I did daily things at home. It stayed conceptual until I hit the road and worked through concepts by way of experience.

This walkabout was for that purpose – or so I thought.

Solo Trek

I got to Albuquerque on schedule, 4:00 p.m., rented a compact white Vibe and drove to an old friend's house. Enjoyed dinner with the family and seeing how happy they were. When they relocated here, the kids were tiny ones, now they were part of our conversation. Ron and I talked while they helped mom, Peggy, clean up. He explained the Navajo people consider Ship Rock, in the northwest corner of New Mexico, the place where people are drawn up into the sky when their bodies die. Also, that there has been three previous events similar to Noah's flood story when masses of Native people were drawn up in a sort of updraft above Ship Rock. I was intrigued.

I slept in my clothes on top of a little boy's bed to minimize my interruption of his sweet life and sneaked out the front door just before 6:00 the next morning. I'd memorized the general grid of the main roads in Albuquerque, so I made my way north, then east towards I-25. There should be coffee and local folk somewhere before I get on the highway.

The first place I pulled off the highway was about an hour up the road; a pueblo Ron suggested last night reflected the orange of sunrise on adobe walls. Car windows down, I drove slowly through their streets trying not to make noise. They were sweeping the dirt and straightening up garden displays for the tourists that would come through later. They looked at me. I smiled back at them. I began to realize this was their home; it was built for families, not tourists. I felt like I was dishonoring their place and soul. My research questions will have to remain in the queue for another time.

Just before I pulled onto the highway, I stopped to consider this adjustment to my intended goal and refocus. The details of this desert quest were not defined, but I felt a discomfort and understood this adventure was not going to be about the usual travelers' agenda. I felt like God's Spirit was trying to get my attention.

God wants me to listen, and trust his directions. I want to see if I really will. Will I listen and obey Spirit over common-sense rationale? Let's see.

I took in a deep breath of dusty air and thanked God for these generations of people who now live in a position of compromise between sacrifice and benefit. On the seat beside me lay an unopened AAA map of Arizona and New Mexico. I looked both ways and turned north.

I smiled as I realized I *did* listen to Spirit and *did* respond.

Now I realized I was here not to get closer to God, but to discover who my true character was in relation to God.

I had intended to find some connection by way of experience between spiritual truths and nature. Plants, animals, gravel, even gypsum. Why are things where they are? How do they reflect God's principles?

I read on the train yesterday that a town named Chimayo was the spiritual center of this area. The Navajo spirit mountain lies west of here quite a ways. I wasn't sure if I'd drive that far, but was eager to see what ever God had for me to see, enjoying the desert's stark beauty on the way.

"Sweet father God. Have I told you lately that how much I appreciate the truth that you can read my mind? Since you can, you know how many times every day I ask you to protect my family. Thank you so much for reading my mind. And thank you for the peace in this car. Void of pressure. Provision for my voice to be audible."

That kind of prayer came easier alone in a car on a road trip. Emotions, whether grateful or tormented, still got stuck in my throat in other environments.

I stopped at a tiny roadside grocery store in Cuba and bought a sandwich for the road. I had no particular lodging target so continued driving north and uphill toward mountains. Just a couple miles farther, I pulled over toward a gravel road that branched off to the east.

I sensed I was supposed to take that road. It wasn't marked, wasn't paved, but I felt sure. I saw on my phone I had signal so I called home just to touch base. I wanted some record of when life ended, if something bad happened. Larry answered but told me to call my daughter, he had to go. I did; she answered. I shared with her how gorgeous the terrain was and a little update on the kids she used to babysit. Did not share what I was about to do.

After our short conversation, I looked over my shoulder to check for any equipment I had for the journey. A wool blanket, tire jack, New Mexico map, bottle of water, and cold sandwich. I evaluated the horizon in front of me: dark clouds along the horizon ahead and late afternoon sun angle behind. Then, I gripped the wheel with both hands and headed my little white car east. I didn't know how many miles it might be before this dirt road intersected a highway, or even if it would.

I drove gravel like I roller skated – careful and alert. Soon, it began raining snowballs. A mix of fog, snow, and rain. Maybe I was in the clouds. This area was between 9,000 and 11,000 feet altitude. The road surface was still okay. Nothing was sticking.

I was in a weird condition. Listening to an upbeat song on the radio, singing "Jesus will be with me all the way," but also scared. It was raining to my left and snowing to my right. I was at least two hours from the nearest town and the dashboard clock said 5:30 in the afternoon. I was still heading eastward into the unknown. Didn't know if the little critter of a car would make it over the mountains without coughing and hacking from low oxygen. I hoped this was a good decision and prayed – tuned in to God being with me and tried to behave accordingly.

Both hands on the wheel, I drove – scared – ahead.

Around a curve, the sun was shining. Beautiful. Now on the other side of the ridge. Red rocks. Red cliffs. Red clay rocks falling off the red cliffs. Horizontal striped mountains.

The wet road descended into a valley. Finally, a sign. Five miles to Coyote; seventeen miles to Abiqu. *Good, maybe a better road at Coyote. I've seen no one else on this road. I'm grateful.*

I stopped and stepped out to take a photo of the whole circular view to the north. The rain here smelled different. Like spring water. Unlike the dusty smell of a Colorado rain, this was almost minty.

One character trait I noticed repeatedly on this trip also played out in my normal life. When environmental conditions were easy on a good stretch of road, I thought, "Oh, I've got plenty of time to explore this or that. Time to go here or there, time to go to Chimayo.

But if I'm thrown a challenge, say it gets dark, dreary, and the road gets curvy, all of a sudden I think, "Oh my, I'm not even going to have time to find a bed tonight. It's going to be cold. I'm going to have a wreck. All that dreadful negative language.

If circumstances change for the good, my responses are positive again. So goes the rhythm of faith and doubt in my mind. Does this mean I lose my faith in every turn of events? Nope. Simply human. But if the battle goes on, I intend to notice my language and fiddle with semantics until it resembles a blessing.

Over those four days in New Mexico, I experienced an unexpected quest. My initial quest was for answers to resolve a religious curiosity. The true quest became to know what character I bring to life.

I know now that I have fear – I know what fear feels like. And I believe God is with me in the middle of my ignorance and fear.

Now, I know my own true character. When faced with scary unknown situations, I stop and take inventory of assets and resources, physical and spiritual equipment. I consider any risks, anchor my life to God's, listen for Spirit, then forge ahead with both hands on the wheel in obedience that voice. No regrets.

I know now to move forward in faith when I'm scared is to be courageous. I have my answer: I'm not a coward. Thank you, God.

Chapter 10: Quantum Kingdom

A Quantum door cracks open

I had gotten a taste of God – a good taste. His Spirit had spoken to me. I'd heard clear statements in or near my head that could only be from God. I'd had nighttime dreams, some that seemed to be from God and seen daytime visions that surely were. Arbitrary people who saw me at church or in prayer groups spoke to me with miraculous precision about my personal life knowing nothing about me. These people spoke under divine inspiration and that was weird to me.

"I have a word from the Lord for you."

This spiritual jargon was foreign to me but descriptive of what came after. I was getting more and more comfortable with that sort of Spirit-powered experience.

I walked wide-eyed in all that weirdness. It was weird that I heard a voice inside and outside of my logical mind. Weird that people I'd never met could nail down the circumstances of my life with clear precision. Weird that I saw scenes so real I might touch them in the middle of a day. Strange happenings, no doubt, but I also had a sense of the truth of it all, and a growing sense of a real God. God who interacted with little ole me.

I knew better who I was, in the character of my soul, but I wanted to know more about God who was the source of all this wonderful weirdness.

Quantum Kingdom

When I read the book of John for data about God, the word Kingdom came up a lot. It seemed interchangeable with heaven: where God lives and where Jesus came from. Unfamiliar with kingdom culture and features like servants, lords, or expected rules of behavior, I wasn't getting the deeper comprehension I was looking for.

Enter PBS. An interview with Brian Greene about quantum theory. In 2011, my ears were just tuning in to this topic. As I understood it, the principles of quantum mechanics govern teeny-tiny particles similar to how our common laws of physics govern ordinary physical things. We generally accept the law of gravity governs falling apples and planetary orbits. The tiny world runs by the laws of quantum physics.

As I watched, Greene's descriptions lit up my brain. I recognized several similarities between quantum theory and the kingdom of heaven Jesus tried to explain to his tribe.

For one, there are multiple dimensions. Maybe seven, maybe eleven, maybe more. Maybe even parallel dimensions where things are going on at the same time but in a different space.

What if one of those dimensions is heaven?

Another principle: we can only see the dimension we live in. Jesus told his tribe, over and over, they couldn't see this other place. Its king was unseeable. Exception: if they saw Jesus, they were actually seeing the king. Weird. At the same time, he urged them to believe weird things about this unseeable place, realm, dimension. He asserted everything he did with them was so people would believe God is, believe that he is God's son, heaven is real, and they could go there.

Another: time is flexible. I had already experienced weird time. Things people told me were spot-on but out of normal linear time. This concept also helped me appreciate my countless déjà vu experiences throughout life.

Another happy concept I latched onto was the observer affect. Mr. Greene explained the double 'slit' experiment and the behavior of particles. They shot electrons toward a wall but designed a barrier with two slits. At first, the pattern on the back wall indicated electrons passed through those two slits like *waves*. But when a camera, or some type of observer was added, the pattern showed particles behaved like individual particles. Adding some type of observer *influenced* the behavior of the particles.

What if this is prayer? What if prayer influences outcome like an observer?

What if the Kingdom of Heaven has physics principles that function specifically there? What if that's what Jesus was trying to get them to understand?

I had been folding clothes, but now I was standing in front of the television, pacing and taking sloppy notes. My face was hot. Finally! I could understand the biblical principles of kingdom in the framework of contemporary science realities. I could adjust and amend ancient vocabulary dealing with this heavenly place, this parallel dimension, and grasp its reality.

I saw quantum theory all over. All over life. All over the bible. It answered some longstanding curiosities, like when Enoch just disappeared – "was no more." I think he did the quantum leap. I learned that when waves of two dimensions come close to one another, some thing in one might pop over to the other. Yes, I realize this is extremely simplified.

More questions emerged, but not frustrating questions. I could accept mystery better these days. And had a comfortable scientific context in which to play with my weird God.

What I know now, I discovered to be true:

Time is linear only for our sake, specific to our dimension, so we can measure our days. I used the phrase *untimed time* in some of these stories because, during some encounters, time was not measurable to me. In many experiences, a prophetic message or a dream happened **before** I had even a hint of any future change. I'm convinced God lives and moves outside our linear realm and the physical rules that maintain it. He exists outside this dimension that includes time, like Sphere existed outside Flatland.

Dimensions Share

By now, the boundary between the physical dimension and ethereal spiritual dimension was as porous as chicken wire. I trusted untouchable images my spirit eyes saw as much as those my earthy eyes saw. Trusted God-audibles more than what my physical ears heard. God's Spirit spoke much clearer.

This Quantum Kingdom dimension of belief was the one I wanted to operate in. In quantum theory, an observer introduced into a particle behavior experiment affected the particle – just by observing. That's weird to my regular mind. But since I'd experienced so many weird God encounters, I chose to believe that theory was as real in the earthy dimension as it would be in God's invisible dimension.

There are plenty of references to mystery in the bible, but the main one I was concerned with was how: people through eons of history connected with an unseeable deity-being. I was tired of living in the emotional mess of rejection, the never-ending demands of life that were so heavy. I wished for a way to connect with the Great Shepherd who cared more for me than anyone here in this dimension.

I recalled song lyrics by Charlie Peacock from the early nineties, "I want to live like heaven is a real place." I really did. I volunteered for the mystery of believing. I would accept with faith whatever mysteries God offered.

For example, it was a Friday night worship held once a month at Harmony Vineyard church. Just as the first song began, I saw a smoky spirit pour down the west wall, seemingly from the stained glass windows about twenty feet high. It flowed across the front of the auditorium between the stage and audience. Then continued back and forth about two miles per hour through the pews with the first measures of music played by the music team. Sometimes it passed in front of the people standing and sometimes it went through them. I wanted to be one whom it moved through, so I bent my left elbow slightly as it came down my aisle. I felt a slight coolness when it flowed through my hand, but only on the downwind side, my palm. Interesting. The spirit cloud settled into the spaces around the folks, seemingly ready to engage.

I came here for the music. To listen, sing, and hope to connect with God. No one oriented or instructed me about what to expect. I came unassuming except for peace. I expected peace and music.

When I saw the stream of smoky fog, no one had to tell me what it was. I knew it was the Spirit. No one else seemed to see it.

It was real. The experience, amazing and warm on one hand, made me acutely aware of my failings. I was – and am not – any angel. I was pretty crazy from the loss of thirty-seven years of effort, wasted love, the pain of rejection. I was mad, loud, and violent – when I wasn't crying. When I lived the compliant wife life, I couldn't even talk to God. But now, even in my mess, I understood he always listens.

What is the deal God? How is it that you communicate with me when I live in sin? What is the truth? Am I living in adoration of You or weakness? Or am I misunderstanding something? How did I get here? How is it that I can't get out of here? Why? Do you want me to depend on you for forgiveness all the time? I'm messing up! Don't you want me to help people? To show them how You fix their hurt hearts? I'm such a sad sample.

In that second, I realized that if my own child was in trouble, I would want to talk to him or her, even in that exact moment of revolt. Even more so if I understood that by cutting off communication, I would contribute to their isolation from my affection that got them into trouble to begin with. I need to understand the scripture that says it's God's lovingkindness that turns a heart away from hurtful living and back to Yahweh.

This logic was the incredible turning point of my journey. Looking at the mess I was in at the time - torn up, volatile, and running – yet knowing more about how God loves, I now understand that situation better. God knew how brittle my soul was, so loved me through the chaos and pain and kept communicating with me.

Conduit Folks

It was another Sunday morning. Spouse and I had what I thought was the ultimate and final great clash. These days it was not unusual to clash but this one was extremely loud and violent. I'd questioned God innumerable times over the last ten years about what this marriage truly was. What God's intention might be with this mess of a marriage? What can one person do by herself alone?

I'd walked away from the denomination we'd been deeply involved with a few months earlier. He, of course, still attended there, sang, smiled, and hugged. I have no idea how he explained my absence.

Avoiding commitment, I found two other church groups. I occupied church seats at services every Sunday, desperate to keep life on track and hoping to get some clue how to survive. One was a casual congregation that had contemporary energizing music and the other one more mature organization with compelling touching music and a preacher that really seemed to care about the real lives of people.

That typical morning, I went to the early service at Harmony Vineyard. From my seat in the balcony, I listened and cried for the half hour of music. Then got in my car and drove to the 9:30 sermon at ReStore Community Church eight miles farther north. On the way there, I prayed desperately, yelling "I can't stand it anymore." Divorce had become a viable option to me a few months ago in April and this was now September. Suicide simmered in the back of my mind at times like this. It seemed a less painful option than living.

I walked like a robot into the building and through the crowd, sat through a sermon on perseverance I tried to hold onto, then walked to my car before bursting into sobs again.

When I arrived back at Harmony, second service music had already started. I took a bulletin from a greeter, slipped inside the glass double doors, stood tight against a strong wooden beam. I thought I'd lean here until break, then go find an open place to sit where no one knew me. I had my notebook out while I stood in the shadows. I hoped to take a few notes about the songs and any message I might be getting through the music to mull over later.

Then Wes Parker, the music leader, ended one song, but before he started the next, he said "I have a word from God for a woman in the back. Over there. Teresa, behind you."

A woman standing two rows in front of me steps aside as he looks behind her at me. I raised my eyes to see Wes pointing at me. I looked to the left, looked to the right, then pointed at myself.

He said, "You. God told me to tell you that you can stand." He said more; my hand took notes but I couldn't stop looking at his face.

When he finished, John Brown, the main leader and preacher, stepped up next to Wes and said, "I'd like to tag onto what you said, Wes. God does not abandon what he has created." John was looking at me. I don't know how many others were looking at me; that doesn't matter. God spoke to me through these two men. They let themselves be conduit for Yahweh and I got the message that God had not abandon me and that I can stand for as long as it takes.

At the break in the service, I found Wes in the crowd of three hundred people in the auditorium. I went up to him and thanked him for his insight. His face was blank. He didn't recognize me; had never met me before. God is amazing. And these two guys allowed themselves to be used by God, interrupt the routine of a church service to save a person's life they didn't even know.

Trouble and pain continued, but I discovered I could stand. That might be all I could do, but I could do that.

Chapter 11: Allies for the Journey
Songs, Dreams, and Day Dreams

Songs as Allies

Singing, my singing, had been ridiculed and restricted in the marriage and in church. Choir had been Larry's main extra-curricular activity in high school and dominated his church life, of course without the sin of instruments. I'd not had that training; my musical training was limited to five years playing flute in a marching band.

I wanted to learn to sing right but he didn't want to teach me. He sang alone or with other guys a cappella. On family road trips, I'd ask that we all sing, but he started songs too high for me and refused to adjust himself or sing something in a lower range.

Songs from hymnals got me through life, but not their melody, not their historical context, not the men's passionate voices. Their lyrics spoke to me like the language of good poetry, symbolic and with deep meaning in the author.

For instance, This World is not My Home – I'm just a-passing through. Farther Along – Tempted and tried, farther along we'll understand why. Jesus knows all about our troubles – but I was still too timid to speak. What a Friend we have in Jesus – I wanted to believe that. Turn Your Eyes upon Jesus, look full in his wonderful face. Love Lifted Me – when nothing else could help. Heaven Came

Down – and glory filled my soul. I had to alter some words to my limited grasp of their accurate meaning.

Things started to open up a bit more with these: Holy Spirit You are Welcome Here, I come to the garden alone, I Can't Even Walk without Holding His Hand, Where the Spirit of the Lord is, there is freedom.

Non-church songs seemed just as spiritual. Amy Grant's lyrics penetrated my heart like my sister's knowing. My Father's Eyes helped me to change my idea of God as father. Lean into the Wind lyrics echoed my perspective on not being a victim to circumstances – after the New Mexico trip.

Charlie Peacock saved my life by his lyrics describing Time is a gift – without time, there'd be no time to change, Heaven is a Real Place – I want to live like that, and Experience – you can only know faith by experience.

Wherever in the millions of songs composed a particular song originated, this is an example of how they transformed me.

♪♪ Beckoning

My brain was already spinning, "What if"-ing around the house. Seeing and becoming more aware of all kinds of repairs that need to be done – all that is unfinished, and all that is unknown about the future. Wrestling with a written – and unwritten – list of decisions to be made.

Should I turn this place into a retreat place to rent out? Is it safe to have strangers in? How am I going to pay the bills? Where else can I find a job?

Allies

I started to do yoga, but only did two poses before I felt the urge to do real work. Got a load of laundry going and straightened the bathroom while pondering.

It was a cloudy day, no radio playing, only sound an occasional distant train horn. Two fawns bound high and happy across the yard, but I have no joy. I'm preoccupied with my mental wrestling. It's aggravating and wasting time.

As I entered the bedroom to strip the bed, a song came forward from the crevices of my mind to my throat before I could think. ♪...when blah blah blah burdens, take it to the Lord in prayer♪

My body froze its motion, I covered my face and cried. In that flash, I realized my Father Spirit had tapped me on the shoulder and turned my awareness toward him. I wiped tears and head to closet central to pray, grateful that Spirit had beckoned so clearly.

I come here to trust You.

"I AM trustworthy."

I come to trust you with the future.

"I KNOW."

Trust you with the details I fret about. Trust you to tell me when. I don't want you to just shine your light on my path, I am blind and stupid, I want You to hold my hand and guide me along Your path!

A second song given me later that morning. In the quietness of a still grey cloudy day, the melody of ♪Love is a Many Splendored Thing♪ joined me in the hallway.

I'm so grateful for your everything! How you communicate with me in a language I can hear and accept. You and I know this language. You penetrate my brain and education to enter my vulnerable heart and speak the truth, inviting me closer, even in all my messiness.

My 1970 Yamaha 150 motorcycle had a thumb switch that, when pressed, released the built-up pressure of the engine. When I drove fast and wanted to seriously slow down and I knew applying the brakes would probably flip me, this pressure release slowed the bike way down fast. This is one way songs function for me; they exhausted pressure that built-up in my soul and simplified things instantly.

I now know that songs turn out to be a precious ally on this quest. Whether a song came from deep memory, contemporary composers, or from Holy Spirit, the lyrics invited me into turns. Turning my mind and heart to walk out new truths in new realities. Some new understanding of my own position, my own value, or a new understanding of the larger situation and my contribution to it.

I keep my spirit-heart in receiver mode. Expecting songs, expecting surprise. Trusting their truth.

Dreams as Allies

As a result of several encounters like this, I was beginning to open myself to the possibility of being loved. What reason, other than love, would motivate God to reach through dimensional boundaries to communicate with me? I knew I did nothing to deserve it.

I've felt that loving communication through strange statements from conduit people. Felt it through songs. And I felt loving communication through dreams. Not necessarily happy scenarios in these spirit dreams, but I considered the warnings and reprimand part of a complete relationship with this king of the quantum kingdom. I was always asking to be shown what I cannot see, so dreams were helpful.

I really looked forward to dreams. Folks who know me well know I do not like to go to watch movies. I don't like putting myself in a receptive position for someone to pour images and ideas into my brain. I don't forget things I've seen, and when I see a film, scenes replay in my mind whether I try to recall them or not. Don't like that.

But dreams from the Holy Spirit were different. These were like little stories that functioned as metaphor, a symbolic comparison to something in fact in my world. A good song describes and helps people understand the complications of life and love in brief lyrics. Dreams and visions from God worked like that too.

January Grey

My dreams were almost always in color. Only stress dreams were monochromatic grey. A typical stress dream was a rope pulled tightly between the sides of my dream-mind periphery, then that taught rope turned into knots that filled my screen, recurring all night.

During the troubling years of this memoir, I was bombarded with extremely vivid and active dreams several times a week. They usually occurred during the hours between midnight and wake-up. I kept a pen and notepad in the closet to record details before leaving the bedroom in the morning, before my mind became distracted by sounds and senses of the day.

God got my attention with a particular series of three dreams in the winter of 2010.

November 5th, God told me the word "January" as I wrote in my early morning journal. That came just before the first of four dreams over the next weeks. As I questioned him what each dream was about, I got more information – or maybe insight. I didn't typically ask God what dreams meant, but this time I asked, "January God? What about January?"

First dream, November 13th: Grey day, flat pastures like the plains of North Dakota, disheveled barbed wire fencing – not anything like North Dakota. A single white centerline on single–lane pavement heading north. I didn't know who was in the vehicle with me but sensed it was my brother, Paul, the rescuer archetype. I felt intense urgency to get over the hill to rescue more rescuers, the hurt ones.

Woke up. Sat with pen, paper and questions in the 40-watt closet. What do I do with this?

"Great and Terrible" he said. "Prepare. Yourself and your soul. Hold to Me. Read Me. Sing now."

The following morning, no dream to record, he told me not to commit to anything in January.

The natural me wondered if my life was about to take a serious turn. I had changed jobs and was teaching two college classes. Thinking

I'd finally found my life's true purpose, I also recalled a bible verse about purpose in Acts: "when God's purpose in his life was fulfilled, David died." What if God was hinting that I would die soon?

I smiled at that thought. *God, that is not terrible, that is luscious! Thank you.*

"Go to sleep; wait for my call. Tune your listening ears."

Next dream November 27th: Grey terrain again. Feels like my car is going to crash; it's not responding well to my steering. I'm transporting a huge all-terrain vehicle filled with nearly a dozen people through heavy construction on a desolate highway – again, northbound. The people were a mix of gender and age, some babies crying but not much emotion in the adults. Their clothes were shredded and wet.

I feel lots of tension trying to get to somewhere. We're heading to some protected place, maybe underground. Not driven by terror, but our motive seems to be the preservation of life.

Then I woke up. I asked God," What are You asking me to do here?"

"One thing: to believe Jesus, my son, is the Way to life with Me."

Next morning, still listening for response to the same question. A fuller reply.

"Walk through these days, listen for My lead each step. Don't look behind; just follow. Walk in the cloud of unknowing. I AM has your hand if you don't fight and pull against Spirit."

Take my hand Yahweh.

December 18th, another awful dream:

Grey world again. Grey rock mountain. I hiked up the north slope, but slope isn't the right word. The whole mountain is only grey slate rock, no vegetation and not very tall – maybe a thousand feet. I'm on the east side of the crumbling path is full of boulders and debris. The trail I'm hiking is narrow, about four inches wide, and is etched into the steep slope of a schist mountain. It looks exactly like the Swiss Alps. The path zigs but I make it.

When I get high enough to see over the rocky peaked ridge, my chest level with the ridge, I see an enormous fireball zoom at a low angle from mid-sky to my left and wipe out the two blocks each side of main street of a town about five miles away. It roared, then rolled, leaving a trail of flaming skyscrapers and raising bright smoke mixed with dust along its path.

Why does it track down a single street? And why does it stop ¾ of the way through the town? Is it a missile? A meteor? Why does it follow along the ground? From my right to my left as I witness the destruction. The four to ten story buildings and businesses along its course are all torn up, smoke and dust rising as I stand helpless.

I falter down the eastern side of the steep, nearly vertical in some places, rock. I try to collect some gentle woman and get her back up that side. It's too crumbly and steep. Tiny people are tucked in crevasses and verbally snip as I pass.

I look down, wondering how I've stayed so stable on this narrow trail. It seems to be only six inches wide.

My feet are not feet, they're hooves. They remind me of my goats' hooves. My hands reach out to my sides and hold onto the nondescript hands of two hooded companions. I even know their names: Solitude and Sorrow. I don't look under the hoods. I'm not curious. We're familiar.

Allies

Dream over. I write details as fast as I can in the dim closet light. Spirit lets me know this is part of the "Great and Terrible"

Sometime that next week, God gave the specific date of Jan 12th. I didn't know what to do. That day was especially busy so I tried to stay particularly tuned in to God, praying as I drove to each of four meetings and obligations around town. I didn't generally do media news, so didn't hear, until the morning of the 14th, that Haiti had had an earthquake.

Was I supposed to have done something? Was this the Great & Terrible thing?

I located a prayer gathering the next week and asked the group what to do when God gives you something. A woman named Daphne told me whether it is local or global, probably what I should be doing is standing in prayer.

Now I get it. That must be what I was doing as I drove through the day on the 12th. Praying off and on all along that day, not even knowing why. God had recruited me to offer spiritual energy in combination with other positive spiritual energy to help people He loves.

What I discovered on this new path of dreams:

Now, I know this grim series of Spirit dreams was not about me. They were messages from the Quantum King who is compassionate energy, operates outside of time, and wanted me to offer my heart. Other people suffer tragic circumstances much worse than what I was in the middle of. Now, when I feel some disturbance in the spiritual sense, I pause, acknowledge some need somewhere, and pray. I don't need to question God for details; details are not my concern. He's asking for my spiritual contribution to a bad situation. If I am later sent, I'll go.

Now, I know not all dreams are messages from God's dimension, but dreams are a valid and mysterious mode of communication obliging my response. If I want to get structured dream interpretation, I'll go to a book, Dream Symbols and Beyond, by Marsha Dunstan.

Synchronicity

One very early morning, I startled awake from a dream. I dreamt I was a boy under water looking up through rolling waves at a man's face leaning over the side of a small boat.

I thought it had to do with my friend Lisa and an organization called Touch a Life in Ghana. Lisa recently posted small bits about a trip there and pictures of Lake Volta. Nothing especially stirred my heart in the description she shared of the local child trafficking issue. A sad scenario of young boys being used as forced labor in the local fishing trade.

I had no idea why this dream came to me. My interest in mission work was limited to orphan homes in Haiti.

I sent her an email and described the dream. Very basic: an eight to twelve year old boy, caught in a net under water, looking up through the water to a sort of master's face.

Lisa replied that she would be coming up from Dallas in a couple weeks for a scheduled house concert. She wanted to chat with me

Allies

when she got to town. I looked forward to catching up with her and her family.

At her concert, a small group of middle aged folks gathered for pizza and to listen to her new songs. Lisa's strong spirit flows out through a tender folksy voice. She shared her faith by sharing the background story of her compositions.

Toward the end of her performance, she sang part of a song she had composed about a boy who drowned while working for his master. Her lyrics didn't match my dream scene, but I didn't expect them to. I replayed tiny details of my dream as she sang. In fact, over the previous two weeks, vivid scenes flashed in my mind while I went about routine activities. For example, while driving to meet girlfriends for Happy Hour, my mind saw a scar – my skin felt the scar – across the left side of my cheek – his cheek – and another longer scar across his left collarbone. The sensation of those scars seemed real and interrupted real time. It also seemed real when I saw the boss-man's face from under water.

After Lisa's last song, she said "Carol, would you share your dream?"

My eyes locked onto Lisa's face and I saw – and felt – the complete scene again.

"The boy's feet and ankles are bound in the fishing net he's been ordered to untangle. The harder he tries to loosen them, the more they bind. He is running out of air and feeling hopeless. Looking up through the water at his earthly master's face, he realizes this master will not help. He stretches out his arms, turns his head to look from his right to his left, and seeing nothing but darkness, embraces the lake, closes his eyes and turns his face upward. He feels welcomed, free and wholly loved by his new master."

I cried. In a way, I am the boy.

Later that night, I located the page where I'd scribbled the dream in predawn light. As I keyed words into the computer, it became a poem. I emailed the piece to Lisa and she replied that she incorporated the poem, I am the Lake, into her song for the remainder of her tour in Nebraska and Iowa.

When Lisa returned home to Dallas, a woman named Jenna emailed a photo to Lisa that she had taken of a young boy from Lake Volta six months before. Jenna lived and worked in Washington State, but was visiting friends in Iowa when she heard Lisa sing the song. When I opened the forwarded photo, I gasped. The scar across this boy's cheek was the scar on the face of the boy in my dream! There was no name for the boy came with the photo.

I had no earthly connection to the woman, Jenna. She didn't know my dream boy had a scar. She didn't know Lisa before her chance meeting at a house in Iowa. She didn't know about Touch a Life in Ghana, or where Lisa's song came from. None of the three of us knew anything except that we'd each been given some part of a whole story and felt compelled to share.

God connected at least four people in this mystical synchronicity: Lisa in Dallas with the voice, Jenna in Washington State with the photo, me in Kansas City with the dream, and the boy in Ghana whose cry God heard.

I don't know if he is alive or drowned. I don't know why Spirit gave me the dream. But I consider this strange phenomenon another invitation to more weird-God events. I don't know if I will ever go to Ghana. I do know that God wants me to pay attention, and there is nothing as wonderful as playing even a tiny part in these extraordinary spiritual connections.

God saw the boy's situation. Did the boy pray? Does it matter? God communicated to me vividly through the dream. What was I supposed to do about it? I don't know. I know I got an opportunity to pray for him and love him, even without knowing his name. God knows his name.

* * * *

I am the Lake

Each time I dive, I join the lake
and swallow its water,
I bite the tangles from his net,
brush against The Man's food.
My slave-brother is Fish.

This day the net's tangles catch me.
I fight, but its knots grip stronger.
My desperate eyes look up
Through the murk, I see my master's stone face
but see no heart or hope.

I've heard of another Master
With food and love for me.

I look left and right in this dark water
and sense – freedom.
My arms stretch out,
I embrace the waters,
Surrender, and rest.

I am the Lake

My end? No.
My beginning.

The new truth I discovered by this turn is that I am a very small person in the world, other individuals are small too. But when we join our spirit to Spirit, God speaks to us, even through us, and amazing things happen. The people in this experience were somehow connected to one another by God's Spirit. I am therefore part of an invisible universe that is so much more than this one dimension.

Chapter 12: Prophetic Milieu

God had done some strange things as he intervened in my painful chaotic marital situation. The marriage continued to come apart, but God continued to show me he was in my life. It felt absolutely crazy when, in one moment, I endured the incredible pain of this bad relationship, and the next moment, God spoke to me or showed me something incredible and caring.

I still had a basic mistrust of people, especially religious people. Even after that "you can stand" experience and I felt positive Wes and John were not speaking from their own agenda. I did believe they allowed themselves to be used by God, but that was not true of the average Christian I'd known.

Prophecy Unpacked

Even the word made me uncomfortable. Maybe because it sounded too churchy. Maybe because I didn't want to be exposed. What if these prophecy people could see all the bad things I'd done? Maybe, I might have to surrender my mind in some way. I wasn't willing to surrender my mind or will to anyone.

When I looked up the word, it seemed pretty harmless: to foretell, predict, to speak under inspiration. The idea of someone speaking under inspiration and telling me the future intrigued me. I sure hadn't done great at predicting my own future. Maybe God could have these people clue me in to what my purpose in living might be. I sure couldn't see one.

My friend, Hannah, had told me she liked to go to International House of Prayer (IHOP) when she wanted to focus on working through an issue. In addition to prayer and worship music, they also provided prophetic sessions we could sign up for online. What if I could get some information, inspired information, from these dedicated people that would help me figure out the mess I was stuck in? I signed up for the first available, 6:00 a.m. on a Tuesday.

The thought of a 24-hour safe place also sounded good to me. I was desperate for a safe place to run to late nights when I couldn't take the frustration of the marriage. I thought I'd walked into heaven when I walked in the big open room. Close to three hundred people of various ethnic heritage, and a broad range of age, sat in the main area; others stood with arms boldly in the air. Dread locks, grunge, or tailored and petite—it was a heavenly rainbow of people.

The music came from a live band on a platform at the front, passionate lyrics, apparently from the bible, or at least with bible language. Not familiar obsolete hymns or currently trending ones, plainly originals from tender hearts. Tears rolled down my silent cheeks.

I arrived an hour before the appointment to calm down and drink in the atmosphere of musicians and singers worshipping and people praying while strolling through the aisles. About fifteen minutes before the appointment, I went to check in, get my number sticker, and sit with others in the back two rows of standard conference chairs in the open auditorium.

In a few minutes, I and two others were beckoned to follow a guy into a small room. Three IHOP people sat opposite us three visitors. One of the IHOP people introduced each of them by first name and explained the scope and purpose of prophecy. From 1 Corinthians 14, they intend their ministry to strengthen, encourage, and comfort. They wouldn't be reading our future. He also said if we had recording devices, they would be happy to speak into them. I had a primitive voice recorder and got it ready.

The first question they asked my group was our names. To break the tension, I told them, "My name is Carol, but you can call me Caleb." I didn't intend it to be a test but I guess it was – for me.

The young woman Angie began.

"When you said your other name was Caleb, I really witnessed to that. Just where Joshua sent out people to check out the land, where many people saw giants, Caleb saw God's potential. I feel you are one that has lived a life of that kind of faith and have had to set your eyes in confidence in what you cannot see and knowing God's faithfulness. I see you as one who has been strong and courageous. That has not feared, has not looked at the natural circumstances. You may have walked through some…a journey of some hard things, physical circumstances, but in the midst of that, you have been faithful to the Lord and remained unoffended. Even with your family in the midst of misunderstanding from your family members, I feel that you really are a testimony to them by the way you live your life. They may not fully communicate that to you but know you are strong witness to them and a light to them. I feel salvation for your family. That the Lord is really doing a work."

This first statement won my heart and welcomed me to listen. Yes, I had lived deeply believing in the unseeable God. I didn't understand God or where I fit, if at all, in God's plan, but I believed. Yes, I had walked through hard physical and emotional circumstances. I don't think Angie was reading that from my face. I began to believe God was telling her these things. Only God could know it. I was glad to hear that God saw I was unoffended. That didn't mean I was weak, but that I truly believe the best of people. I believed when people hurt me, they surely didn't do it intentionally.

"Also, just provision. Provision of finances. The Lord has heard your cry. Isaiah 55, that every word spoken, what was sent out to accomplish a thing will not return void. It will water those seeds of intersession that have gone up. You will see the fruit of your labors, those who sow in tears will reap in joy. In the midst of the trudging through the wilderness, just like the Israelites, you are coming into a time of rejoicing and entering into the promises. Coming into the promised land and seeing that lush place. You have been trudging in a wilderness and will start seeing the flowers blooming and seeing prayers being answered."

I hadn't thought about finances, but I figured if financial issues were on God's radar, these people would be given a "heads up" so I paid attention. I loved that she acknowledged my history of trudging. It made me believe God witnessed my perseverance, and that made me cry. Someone knows what I've been through!

Ken: "I see this long winding road, a big wine glass at the end that is the Holy Spirit joy of the Lord. I see him giving you great joy. It's been a hard ride. When you go around those winding turns, you never know where you're going to end up. He is bringing you joy."

I'll take it! I'll take that glass of Holy Spirit joy wine! He was so right about the unpredictable turns and the hard ride.

Jeff: "I'm getting Song of Solomon 4 and 5. Your heart cries 'I just want to love you more, I want to love you the most I can.' And right now with all the tribulations and pressures and trials that are going on, they're going to be there all your life. Don't get a wrong perspective on them. He is going to send a north and south wind on you. You are a woman of refreshing and of awakening and He's doing that in your life. He's saying I want you. I'm putting you in circumstances to awaken your heart even more. Don't get a wrong perspective. You've had an accepting attitude of un-offense in your heart. You've not let those things stay there. In James 1, I'm letting these things mature and perfect you to produce love within your heart. He's answering every cry of your heart. He's saying don't be offended by things I'm sending your way. 2 Corinthians 4-5, the Lord's saying you're going to carry My life and death in the same moment. You're a vessel filled with His glory. There are pressures and circumstances to push you, but you're not crushed. He's not abandoned you in any way, but there's light manifested in you. The Lord is going to make you an awakener. You're going to awaken people's hearts to love. You're going to speak healing and deliverance over their lives. Preach messages that call people to consecration and to purity in their own life. Many who have fallen back and believed a false grace message. You're going to be such a rock of faith in your circumstance. You're going to say, "This is what the Lord is!" And many will say, how can you know this in the midst of your pressures?

Really? Tribulations and pressures all my life? You, God, love me and are going to put pressures on me because you love me? You're going to make me an awakener? What does that even mean? I actually love the part where Jeff told me God would not abandoned me. I hold tight to that idea. I've had enough abandonment for one life.

Angie: "I immediately got the word: forerunner for you. Even like Jesus went before us to follow. I saw you driving in your car on a road and there's a map with key points on it. You're going from place to place but going before. Going before to prepare the way, like John the Baptist going before, preparing the way. Feeling pressure from things that are hard is in part from that place of being called to go first, before others get it, before others have built it."

I'm always driving. I've always got a map. My little sister calls me "Scout." It seems natural for me to go places other than where normal people go. But I never thought that might be part of who God made me to be. Of course I am familiar with the touch of anxiety that comes with breaking a trail; that helped me understand what Angie said about pressure from hard things being part of going first. Will I be assigned to break some sort of spiritual trail so other folks can travel it easier? I can accept that assignment.

You have an anointing on your life to build, and to be there at the beginning to build up so others can follow. I feel courage and boldness. The Lord says you are a woman of courage, you are a woman of boldness, go with boldness. And when you are driving in your car, the Lord is with you, sitting beside you.

I loved the idea that Jesus or the Holy Spirit rode in the passenger seat on road trips. I wouldn't depend on him to read the map or navigate, but sure would enjoy conversation with him in that atmosphere.

"You've walked in this already but he is going to awaken even more your reality of the bridegroom. He is the bridegroom. When you go before, ahead of people, even if you feel the pressure or the difficulty of being the one who builds, the one who steps out breaks out of the mold, out of the crowd to go forward and build, to walk with the Lord in the way he is walking. I feel the revelation that he's your bridegroom; that He is with you, you're not alone, He is your husband, forever betrothed to you, forever with you in every situation."

God knows my intent to be close to him. He is my husband. Just a few days before this, I was sleeping on the couch – again – and woke up alert at four in the morning. I walked around the corner to the dining room, turned on the light and sat down in front of an open bible. I fanned a few pages and stopped at a verse I'd never seen before. Isaiah 54:5 …for your Maker (Creator) is your husband. Yahweh is his name and he is God of all the earth. Of course, I cried happy sobs. This girl Angie had no way of knowing that unless she was tuning in to Yahweh God.

"I just feel the reality of that coming to you, more than in words, more than anything you've ever experienced before, that the presence of the Holy Spirit, the presence of the bridegroom on your life is going to be magnified. To know that in pressure or anything you go through, even in joy, just to lean on the bridegroom, knowing that he's there, and He is with you. And I do feel an anointing of finances over your life, God has his finger on you in that area.

Ken: "Yeah, I got the word awakening too, and I felt like God is really just awakening you in this season where you're going to be able to understand more of the invisible realm. He's going to open up your mind and begin to understand how the things of the invisible realm, how they affect the visible realm and vice versa. And just a lot of spiritual warfare there and he's just gonna open up your mind and you're gonna begin to understand. That's all I had with that….Um. Do you farm by chance?

I nod and reply that I have a big yard and grow a little food, a lot of herbs mostly.

"Alright, uh, Lord, bless that. Okay. Yeah, Lord I would ask that you bless what she does in that arena; open it up as a ministry and bring others alongside her. Bless her. Bless Carol in Jesus' name."

Jeff: "It seems like this summer is a season of encounter with the Lord. That in some pretty important challenges, the Lord is going to visit you in some special ways. Encounter your heart but also give some direction with things. And like Angie said, you're going to be building things. I feel the Lord is going to give you some education and business things, you're going to come in and give counsel to them, like godly wisdom to them. Where it used to be a secular thing, it's going to fall under a structure where you're going to encounter some of that. Involved with business and buildings and even the education realm as well."

That summer, I started an LLC to buy properties for delinquent real estate taxes. I'd forgotten this message in the stress of living, it didn't seem as immediately relevant as the other insights these three conduit people were offering in the moment.

Angie: "I got James 1:27 where pure and undefiled religion is visiting widows and orphans. I saw something about the inner-city, orphans and children, maybe troubled teens. I saw you being an insight to them. Maybe you have a vocation, I saw you teaching a vocation or a skill that they need to come out of prostitution, to build so they have a direction for their life."

This proved to be confirmation that my place of employment for the next two years was the right place for me to be. Three weeks later, I was hired as a job coach with City Union Mission. Yes, inner city. Yes, I taught clients vocational skills. And many were orphans, whether 17 or 65, and I got to love them.

"Also, I just kept getting the story of the woman who had an issue of blood. She broke through the crowd to touch the hem of Jesus. The Lord says do not fear the crowd. Break through the crowd to touch Jesus. And I got this phrase: let hunger be your compass, the thing that guides you. You're in a season of walking in hunger as the thing that guides you and as your compass. Even as Jeff was saying, as a season of encounters, even in your forerunner calling of building and all that, just to encourage you in the way that God sees you, that you are courageous and bold, have no fear of breaking away from the crowds to touch the hem of Jesus' garment.

Yes, I was hungry. Hungry for heaven! Someplace good and not chaotic or painful. But what I was most hungry for was to know the truth about who this God is. Why does life hurt so much? Do I even matter to anyone? Where are the answers? I'd already committed to eating crickets and wearing burlap if God would please just show me the truth. Angie's words encouraged me to keep on asking questions and keep on hunting.

Prophetic

Ken: "How is your back? Is your back okay?

"It's okay. No problem."

Okay, fine. It was really just a question. I just saw a spinal column, but if it's fine I'm not giving you any back problems."

Ken sensed a problem with my spine – spinal column. He prayed for my healing and asked me to let him know if I felt anything. Maybe Ken saw the wounds in my back from the fiery darts that Jeff told me about!

Jeff: "I feel like there have been heated arguments and words nailed into you. A spirit of accusation comes at you through those words, that they were put into your heart, but like not from the Lord. Was there something spoken that you remember, maybe a harsh statement?

I replied, "Many."

Okay. Well Lord we just thank you for Carol. Take out those fiery darts from her back, Lord, and from her heart. We say "be gone in Jesus name." we speak healing into her heart, all those words. We ask that You break that spirit of rejection and anger and torment that will come over her. Torment over relationships bring fear of intimacy in relationships with family and friends. They bring fear of pursuing the Lord with your whole heart. And speaking; just break out of that lie that says you can't speak the truth, that you can't speak the whole truth to anyone the Lord highlights.

Yes. I lived in "duck and cover" mode for a long time. Everything I did and said was misinterpreted, judged wrongly and used against me. But I didn't really want to know specifically who was backstabbing me with false accusations. I loved my family, all of them. And even if I knew who, calling her or him out was not going to stop it or change their attitude. Only God could do that. I still pray. It's still going on.

Angie: "Speak of freedom Lord. I pray that the spirit of adoption be released God. That she is accepted in the beloved. Help Carol know You are not disappointed with her. Heal her Lord. Bring her peace and restoration and healing, I pray that there be healing. I pray even tonight as she goes to sleep Lord, I pray for an encounter, a dream, visitation, an increase of the angelic around her."

This prophetic session and others that followed did help me believe God was not disappointed in me. A couple other sessions even began with someone telling me before we even got started, "God wants you to know He is pleased with you!" God knows I need to be reminded.

Jeff: "Lord, for her family and her brother that there would be manifestations of your power, that he would call and ask questions. There be reconciliations, convictions, and dreams released into her family and friends right now. Come, I ask You this week that there be testimonies, Lord. We ask that You do these things Lord, tonight and tomorrow, that people would be calling her and apologizing, would be repenting, be getting saved, Lord. Healed and delivered Lord.

No one called, asked questions, or apologized. No one repented that I know of; maybe they're still being healed and delivered. God's time is not our time.

Angie: "Abba, I ask that Carol would know Your presence. I pray that any pain in her heart, any residue of loneliness in her heart, that it would be gone, that she would know the presence of the Holy Spirit. Lord, we just speak from this point forward, that she would walk in the unity of God, knowing that she is not alone. That she would be so confident in the fact that she is not alone. Give her the gift Your presence, of tangibly feeling and knowing and walking with her Father-God, with the Bride Groom.

I ask Father that you would mend pain from the past; that she would be able to look back and see exactly where you were and what you were saying. The way You were carrying her, Your words of Truth that You speak over her. Lord, I pray that even now, the voice of the Shepherd, that every memory would be filled with the voice of the Shepherd, the truth of the Shepherd, even now the voice of the bride groom. Bless our sister Lord. Let her hear You so clearly."

Jeff: "I ask for a wall of fire to surround her. We command every spirit that would torment her, that would accuse her, to be bound and be moved from her body and from her life, in the name of Jesus. And we say go. Go. In the name of Jesus. We plead the blood of Jesus over her body. We thank you for her life, we thank you for her calling, for her heart, her personality. We thank you that You have placed her in this time, Lord. Thank you for Carol. Thank you for Carol. A blessed sister. She will never die. You will never die Carol. You'll have a brand new body that can live forever. You will live forever; you are sowing your body, sowing your life as a grain of wheat."

This session lasted seventeen minutes on my audio recorder. It seemed to move like waves of the ocean on the beach for me. Each assessment or point one of the people spoke had the force of a wave, a crashing awareness in my mind of the issues in my daily life that these kind people could not possibly be aware of, unless the Spirit of Truth informed them. But I knew – I knew what they were talking about. Not in detail. They didn't call the name of my brother-son-father-man when they spoke of his issue. I knew his name. I knew his issue.

They didn't say specific accusations, fiery darts, stabbed me in the spine. Why would they? God knows. And the purpose of these ministers, like they explained, was to encourage, strengthen and comfort, not to place blame. I was encouraged to keep on trudging through this messy life. I was comforted to know that God knew the unfair abuse I'd taken. He knew the abusers. He knew the damaging blows my heart had taken. They said I'd have troubles and pressure all my life, and I felt stronger to face them knowing I wouldn't be abandoned by God. And I had never been abandoned. Ever.

How did this change my relationship with God? It demonstrated more of the loving father character of God to me, but also made it clear God knows the deepest invisible distress. He cares about me. He knows the pain in my heart caused by family nailing accusations to my back. God knows everything. He didn't place blame on the hurtful ones – or me.

My faith turned dramatically during this single prophetic session. I walked out of that place feeling deeply and authentically loved for the first time in my life. I began to accept that God was pleased with me. Even if I didn't work my fingers to the bone, even if I misunderstood him, even if I failed at something. He knew me better than I knew myself and loved me anyway. My response was a sense of freedom to love God even more, truly loved, I could reciprocate without reservation.

I still lived my regular life, but at the same time, acknowledged these 'weird' God intersections. As troubling circumstances came to me, I recognized the Spirit's explanation of events addressed the situation from a heavenly point of view.

This experience was a critical turning point, and I now know this to be true:

Prophecy operates like ovaries. Eggs come to maturity at different times, exploding from their ovary when the right time has come. They grow and bulge at the edge, then burst, releasing with energy to make their way through open space, space between dimensions, to the next pathway, onward toward fulfillment of purpose. These prophecies matured and burst forth at unique unpredicted rates. One spoken In April burst forth the next year September.

The thing about prophecy is that it didn't change my circumstances – not exactly – but did cause me to respond differently to circumstances. I didn't, I can't, comprehend how my problem fit in the huge web of relationships over time and geography. I do accept the idea that God doesn't take sides, and I believe he wants good for all.

Chapter 13: What About Us

The Main Thing

Early October of that same year, two girlfriends and I drove about an hour north of town to harvest grapes at a small vineyard. An enjoyable Saturday event on a cold fall day. Laughing, bonding, and a nice lunch provided by the vineyard in appreciation for our work.

I drove separately so I could head west afterward and stay overnight at the monastery I occasionally retreated to. I left about three o'clock, but oddly didn't feel real strong about my decision. Drove to Atchison anyway, approximately forty minutes west, but kept an open prayer mind while I enjoyed occasional wildlife sightings on the back roads.

My usual place to sit and breathe there was a thick wood and iron bench in the open area thirty feet from the cliff above the Missouri River. Grass is groomed, sidewalks to the monastery are vacant. The view of tree tops across the river and the ever-rolling Missouri invited me to spend some time. The sun had descended, and while I tried to figure out if God wanted me to stay or not, the full moon rose.

Then I heard the Spirit of God. "Follow the moon."

"What?"

What About Us

"Follow the moon like you follow Me"

Oh, my. I let it soak in for a minute, then responded calmly to what I heard. This is not normal, but I got the directive clear as a bell. I scan the Missouri dimming treescape across the river to the east and establish dusk coming on. No time to hesitate. I picked up my books and hustled to the car.

I guess I'm not staying overnight tonight. Glad I didn't check in.

A few blocks down the hill, I turn east over the bridge; the full moon is directly ahead and still low in the twilight sky.

I wondered if this is like when the wandering people of Jewish history followed the pillars of fire and smoke all over the wilderness. I like this adventure so far.

I'm not yet considering how far I will go with it. In this moment, I am simply doing it. Sort of meditating in a condition of compliance. Normally, I'd have a map in the car door's pocket, but I understand that is not part of God's trust challenge this day.

The first road out of town ran east but gently curved around these Missouri hills, so when the asphalt highway came to a T, the moon was to my left. I simply turned left, following the moon. A right turn would take me back to Kansas City on familiar roads. I felt a familiar bit of adrenaline and smile. St. Joseph was this direction so I could just go that far and head home if I wanted to.

Just a couple miles up that highway, the moon was now on my right and a gravel road presented its opportunity. My brain argued against turning onto strange road into a darkening sky.

"I can always turn around."

I wanted to go farther into this experience of trust. Following the verbal direction of God into unknown. Maybe it was just roads, turn by turn, but I set aside measuring any outcome; set aside my typical planning options. This drive was simply my response to God's voice.

I wanted to see what happened if I did this obedience thing, such a private encounter. Four or five miles, driving directly toward the moon. Boldly, I pressed God, "What do you want me to do with this?"

God pressed back, "The main thing."

"Crap." I might have known what he meant but didn't want to acknowledge it.

"You can't avoid it. Deal with it."

The road came to another T-intersection. I turned right, but the whole next mile, I pouted. I realized what God meant by The Main Thing. My crappy marriage. I knew I was supposed to do a forgiveness thing – to be forgiving. I'd gotten the message to "show mercy" when I asked what to do with this jerk I'm married to. And I'd gotten the message to write the story, but such a painful story?

"The Main Thing."

"Okay, okay." I agreed and felt my shoulders relax.

I recognized the road I was on, not the physical road, the spiritual road. It would be difficult, but that's okay; I've dealt with difficult tasks before.

Over the next hill, familiar lights of an interstate highway ramp invited me to drive home.

That evening's trek was *not* a pointless meander. Obedience was on the table, I obeyed. But trust was on the table too. God compared himself to the moon, an ever-present light to focus on during a dark journey. I'd trusted the moon to be visible during this dark night. Will I trust God to be as present as this moon had been through this next, even tougher, trip?

This mysterious encounter convinced me God's Spirit would be as constant as that moon. I also learned I couldn't dodge the Main Thing by turning away or down side roads and distractions; the issue, the problem, would also be as constant as that moon.

This turning point didn't fill me with joy, but delivered a solid new truth to walk out with. It was a strange night drive, uncounted turns, and a private lesson in obedience taught by a Spirit-whisperer. The important thing that turned was my will.

Retirement

He'd been retired for two years and was still not engaged with me or life here. He offered the same phrase for decades to calm me down, "Just hang on for a couple years. Things will get better."

I thought that qualified as a promise so kept hoping, even though he told me he never made promises. He and my Mom laughingly agreed promises are meant to be broken. Whatever they meant by that, it didn't help me understand what they were actually saying.

I was trying to talk to him about a conflict between two married friends.

"He's a better avoider than I am." He slid that statement out as a compliment.

My body shivered, prickles. Not initially anger, but a remembrance and replay of so many memories. I walked out to the kitchen, then came back in to say, "That is not a good thing. Is this something we can talk about?"

No response.

I wondered what his reason for even saying that was. Such a hurtful statement, such a stupid thing to say just to get to me. He sat in his boxers in the recliner through the morning. When I came back in from the garden, he was still there, I was still upset.

"Did you say that so I would say he's not as bad as you or you're not as bad as him?"

I don't know if he intended manipulation, but this felt like trickery. Manipulation on his part? Maybe justification of himself? How can I know when he won't engage and clarify? Again, I'm left to stew.

Senseless statement. What did he want me to do or say? Was it an opening to another topic? Was he jerking my chain, trying to get me involved in something, or try to justify himself, maybe fishing for a fight or a compliment, I don't know. This is our history – again and again.

My gut was a mess. I don't know what I'm supposed to do when I'm being controlled, pushed and shoved by other people; don't like being married to him. I do surrender to you God, I surrender to you God.

What about hate?

Robbie Dawkins is a deep believer in God healing people for the simple purpose of expressing God's true love. The church scheduled him to speak and pray for people's healing. He invited folks to walk around one of the rough areas of Kansas City to pray people get healed and know God wants a relationship with them.

I had always related to outcast folk and really wanted to go along, wanted to be with others who seriously cared for them too. However, I still hadn't conquered the hatred I had in me toward the husband who'd done so much to hurt me.

When Robbie finished speaking and the prayer team had spread out along the front of the stage, I walked up to Sam, a young man about twenty who I'd seen pray with others. I got my first excuse ready, "I really want to….." the rest of it was supposed to say: go with you guys but I hate my husband, but I was cut off.

Robbie's full-bodied presence appeared from nowhere, bent forward from atop the stage, and pointed his finger right at my face. "Hate does not disqualify you!" He repeated it and prayed for me.

How did he even know that was what I was going to say? It had to be God! Did Robbie read my mind? Or did God's Spirit use Robbie to set the truth upright in that moment?

That statement rooted a new truth and turned my previous logic upside down. What changed in me was that hate could no longer function as an Impenetrable barrier between God and me. My feelings of guilt, the weight of self-condemnation needed to be set aside in order to care for people. I loved God and wanted to serve Him, but thought I wasn't qualified *until* I eliminated the hate in me.

Robbie also said – looking me square in the eyes – the hatred will fall away as I get on with working for God. Also that I've had some hurtful, even slanderous things said about me and to me and he is sorry. He prayed for healing. He held my head and prayed.
I'd been trying my hardest to overcome that pain for most of ten years. God knew that. That wall of belief was knocked down in a moment. I could love people *more* than hate the spouse. More love in the space of my heart and soul, the less room for hate of any kind. From that turning point moment, I was freed up to love. Freed to focus on love. Freed to give hate no attention.

Labyrinth

Chapter 14: Labyrinth Reprise

Labyrinth Reprise

Let's circle back to the labyrinth experience to make sense of these contradictory situations. I began walking in the literal world, but transformed into an ethereal world. Reality shifted.

Why did I come? I have a hunger to know; not about society or trending subjects, but I stepped into unknown because I thought I'd know God better. One of my cousins has lived on a sailboat for over two decades. By stepping into her boat, I learned more about her. I thought stepping in to this simple labyrinth would help me grasp a spiritual facet of the Deity people have been drawn to over all of history.

I wasn't looking for another wizard or a prepackaged ideology that fit like a nice robe; I was looking for the real thing. I trusted scripture to be an introduction. I should have no reason to fear.

I had no intention to predict outcomes; that's not me. I offered myself to the moment. Had no awareness of temperature, wind, or time. I came away from this exercise interpreting my life radically different.

What I vocalized (and didn't) inside the labyrinth surprised me. Recounting my sad history had become habitual. But there seemed no need to detail a pain-filled life in here; God already knew every detail. However, I felt a massive desire for God simply to be in the situation, recognizing his Being is good. I felt God's holiness AND intimacy. That was totally unexpected. My deepest desire was to be one with this One.

Before the labyrinth, God was authoritarian. That perspective brought with it shadows and reminders of dread and guilt. Afterward this engagement, I recognized God as holy, majestic beyond comprehension, with deep intimacy illogical in the regular world.

Nothing about the labyrinth physically changed, I did. My mindset really was different after each turn. Before walking this grassy path, my mind wandered about lots of topics from a church environment or read in scripture. But once I encountered the turn, like a particular vision or God-audible, all my pre-turn conundrum was satisfied.

Truth that satisfied my troubled mind about a situation for my life, for that time. I didn't wonder if I deserved it; didn't wonder if it would happen again, didn't wonder if it's the same for everyone. Nope. It happened to me. It happened and gave me truth. Truth for me. Truth for now.

God showed me the truth of generosity even though, from my perspective, I had nothing to offer. The vision of water flowing into my palm and overflowing is God's truth.

The labyrinth experience removed the overwhelming sense that life's chaos was just too much. Chaos inside me even when my outside was quiet. This experience taught me the truth of oppositional realities that can take place at the same time and in the same space. Because of a multidimensional coexistence like a physical labyrinth and a spiritual experience, I discovered I can live in spiritual peace inside even when terrible things happen in my earthy world.

I could accept as true that even with the incredible pain of my precious family exploding, God's truth that I had a strong family.

It was not fun, walking the labyrinth, or walking these last years with the Spirit. It has been intense and full of wonder.

A labyrinth became a representation of my life. I know now I just need to keep walking. My path will turn at least once more. Some odd event will transform my current line of thought, and if I hold as true that the unseen spirit is real, I'll grasp a new spiritual truth - and I won't see it coming.

Chapter 15: Released

Mom-God debunked

As I fell into my bed the day of their arrival, my heart hurt for them.

Four days of hard driving for this 82-year old gentle man with his 78-year-old wife alongside had spent them both. They got to my house after lunch and moved their stiff bodies from their van to the kitchen table for hot tea and cookies.

It was work to listen to their recap of stories over the last year. Stories that didn't match. Bob's eyes looked tired. I wondered how weary he was from the drive and how weary he was from life with Mom. I was glad to have them here, but felt so sad. Sadness mostly in response to my mother's mannerisms.

Mom's mouth pinched into an 'O' with that continual scowl now supplemented by a twitch. (I remember what it was like to live with this scowl. Scowl aside, her nonsensical comments, cutting verbal digs, and flinging of her hands cinched my diagnosis of dementia.

Maybe she's just stressed from the long trip. Or has she always been a bitchy, demanding, mouthy woman? Aging traits like weakness or pain could be more tolerable or manageable if she would just accept them as part of the present. Instead, she flings her hands, cusses, and blames Bob, my stepdad, for everything. None of these things were new, they were just more apparent than last year.

After supper, they retreated to the room we set up as their little home base for the time they'll be here. We're planning to look at houses for sale so they can move here. My offer, husband agreed, Mom and Bob sounded excited on the phone.

In my bathroom, behind closed door, I ask, "God, what do I do with this? Is this also my fate, my genetic code? Please help me stay pleasant with a smile for my family. And God, thank you so much for the forgiveness my kids offer for my own scowling face in their past. I am so grateful."

"Now forward," is what I heard Spirit say.

Okay. Forward. How does it apply? Leave the past. This is now.

They have come to consider the possibility of moving here from Washington State to be close to family who would care for them when they need it. I determined to view my parents' extended stay with an observer's eye and evaluate their aging state, mental and physical health from an objective perspective.

But after only two days, observing their aging status turned personal – and personally ugly. My early-morning prayer time has produced a list of what I'd given up instead of peace and patience. I feel trapped, bound, bored, irritated, set up, overwhelmed, burdened, frustrated, sad, and confused.

I was not prepared for all this, nor did I want this job! Take note: these was my selfish mind. The more I thought about the situation, the more scared I got. Scared my soul would be swallowed up by these elders. To sit – and I hate sitting – and listen to her redundant negative stories, and try to converse and make sense of them seemed so futile, a waste of time. Mom's never-ending put-downs of her siblings and the people of our hometown make me crazy. I left home at eighteen, yet I think my compliant child's mind was still trying to believe her crap. My adult mind, weakened and stunned, didn't care about ancient lies and gossip, but at the same time, didn't want to hurt her feelings. My mind spun like an engine given gas while its gears in neutral. My voice is blocked.

Released

They didn't ask one thing about what their visit might disrupt. Is it my error to value my life? I've worked hard to build something spiritual, intellectual, and productive. I didn't know how to or how much of my life to preserve. What do I do? Joy and freedom were precious to me, yet I loved these two. I'd always set aside my own life to do what Mom asked me to do for her. She's my mom.

How frail these two. How near the end of life. Why can't I ask the questions I need to? *Why won't you walk more, Mom? Do you understand what is going on with your health?* She hides in her solitaire, at first with a smile, then with a frown, back to a smile and brags that she cheated to win the game. *Great. This is my bloodline.*

I just wanted to go away somewhere and blow off steam. Drive to the trail by the river and just run. In this fantasy, I'd return refreshed, a bit physically spent but calm enough to deal with this boredom. Assuaged enough to tolerate nonsensical dialog.

On the other hand, what must they feel like? They have a home three days drive from their children and grandchildren. Their neighbors and friends pack up and leave for the winter months every year. They've had health scares; Bob's heart bypass surgery and a hip replacement that got permanently infected. Mom has vague "spells." Whatever those spells are, Bob is worried and tries his best to help her out of them.

"She gets confused and cantankerous," he says.

God, please tell me what to do, how to think. You told me to accept things as they are when you said "Now forward" but can you tell me more? Overall, I have peace about their phase of disengaging from life, but what am I supposed to do with them? Can you provide some wisdom? What can I do to help?

Ben, my middle son, brought his family over for lunch to see his Gramma and Grandpa. During lunch Mom is reserved, conversational, and calm. She asked Ben normal update questions and listened to his answers. She had not moved from that dining room chair since before breakfast five hours and several cups of coffee ago.

As I offered Ben's wife, Tracy, a cup of hot tea. Mom wagged her finger at me from her chair across the room and barked, "You'll need to stir that because the cinnamon has settled to the bottom."

I'm silent and confused; this tea is in teabags. She must be thinking of the dry Russian tea mix she made when we were growing up. I tell her it's okay and continue to fix lunch. A few minutes later, I notice she'd disappeared from her morning perch. I find her in her bedroom alone playing solitaire. She doesn't answer my questions, just snaps, "I'm gonna take a nap."

Is this the short term memory loss of dementia? Does she know what is going on? How can she stay oriented in the present when she spends such a great amount of time sleeping; napping throughout the day?

She woke up an hour later and first thing, called Bob in from the shop. He came inside, back to their room where she chewed him out. "You were yelling at me in my dream! I want a divorce!"

"Oh Honey, you just had a bad dream." He calms her and leads her to the table for afternoon coffee and more cookies.

Later, Bob and I went shopping for Alka Seltzer. As soon as we got in the minivan, I asked, "Does Mom forget things?"

He jumped in, "Oh, yes! Sometimes she's worse than others. Sometimes she's bad for almost a week."

He goes on to say their family doctor suggested Bob "dole her pills out to her" every day. She forgets. And this woman is paying their bills?

Her scowl was perpetual. I remembered the first time I ever saw Mom smile I was eighteen. She and Bob were newlyweds. In her older years, she only smiled at Bob if she was pleased with something, otherwise it's a scowl.

Released

These days, she adds mouth twitching, one of those twitches described in the list of Lewy dementia symptoms I read.

We looked at houses after I got off work in the afternoons and every weekend for the month they stayed. Bob liked several; Mom liked none. It was always the bathroom she had issue with. Bob offered to remodel, and we would help. Then, early one December morning, they announced with coffee they were going home. They had watched the weather and were going to try to beat a blizzard heading their way. That made no sense. It would take them four days to drive back to Washington and the blizzard coming off the Pacific forecast to hit Washington in two. Whatever logic they used, it was rock-solid to them.

My daughter was due with her second precious baby the next week. Mom had told her she was glad they would be here for the birth. They loved Leah. Leah was glad for them to share such a cool event. How would I explain their leaving to her?

They must have started in the middle of the night. Their room was already packed up, bed neatly stripped. All that was left to do load the van. They'd been here a month so it took a long time to load and organize their vehicle. Bob and I carried bags and boxes, Mom pointed and ordered what went where. She swayed her three-hundred pound mass back and forth, then hobbled around the tailgate and toward the front passenger door. He opened it for her and helped her crooked fingers get a grip on the seat. He patiently held her cane while she grunted and cussed. "This goddam van."

Bob was aging at 82, but was not frail of body or mind. He loved Mom. He loved us, and would have adapted well to this new place. I assured him I'd support him and see what resources we might find in their area of Washington to help. I'd help, but I had a job and family here, married adult kids and a growing herd of sweet grandkids.

Obligatory hug from Mom; long solid hug between Bob and me. They drove up the hill.

That was a Saturday, so without work scheduled, I had time to consider what had just happened before I would call the kids to explain the change. I heard what Mom said but knew it was not the truth of the big picture. I wanted to hear from God. Connect with and commune with the Holy Spirit. Because of my routine of sitting with him in the dark hours of my mornings, I knew God-Yahweh was familiar with my inner being. And I trusted him to care for my spirit in this turmoil and give me truth.

I huddled in my closet with pen and journal to listen. Internal tension built up those last weeks like a path segment in the labyrinth that lead up to a 180° turn. And like labyrinth turns, I walked out of the turn with a different mindset. Reality will be changed.

Truly released – turning point

That short month opened my eyes. I had idolized Mom my whole life. I'd come to her aid every time she called me. Every - single - time. It never occurred to me to refuse her need. I'd always believed she worked way too hard, only wanted the best for her family, and knew what was best for me. I still deeply loved her, loved them both, but during those weeks, I saw her differently. Because of dementia weakening her just a little, a veil was lifted for me to see through. She was mean spirited, by nature. She manipulated, ridiculed, lied, and always bragged that she'd won. She wanted to be the one and only star of the show and Bob and I were her puppets to make that happen.

I still felt like a puppet; but a puppet whose strings had been severed. I'd been cut free from Mom. I started to think I'd lost my mother, then realized I'd just released her as my god.

Mom always thought she was pretty special. I did too. She didn't understand anyone denying a directive for what she might want. I didn't realize I could

Released

opt out, ever. My sense of unescapable surrender to her power was now gone.

So many scenes replayed in my memory as I processed this new reality. Mom was not my puppeteer.

On my visit the year before, as soon as I walked in the door after a three-hour flight and five-hour drive, she called a friend to come to the house and give me a permanent. Mom had already paid the woman $20. I protested but ended up yielding to her will. It would have been an even longer week than it was if I hadn't. That won't happen again.

She commanded me to dig something out of the massive chest freezer for supper. She pulled up a chair ready to comment on each item I withdrew. I didn't even get one package out before she began her rant, "…the real problem in the family history is that ___ isn't even ___'s father. ___ was sleeping around when he was gone." I'd heard all these stories multiple times over the last forty years, I didn't want to hear it again. But I stood at attention, my body toward the open freezer but my indifferent face toward hers. She rolled her eyes, huffed, and shook her head radically when I didn't respond.

She didn't really want conversation. She just wanted to be center stage, exalted and revered as the source of the secret truth. That power was gone.

I'd always tried to make her world better. We had a small grocery store for a year, trying to salvage the farm that Dad gambled away. She did the butchering and wrapped meat in the back room. I ran the cash register, delivered groceries, and stocked shelves after school. I cleaned and mopped the floors after we closed at 8:00. Sometimes I slept on those clean floors because school came early.

I was seventeen. I kept a flannel night gown handy. It had tiny flowers and tiny ruffles around the chest panel. I kept it handy because I didn't really know where to sleep anyway. The farm was ten miles north and not safe. The car wasn't safe either. Mom and Dad divorced the year before and it was ugly. Mom was dating Bob and she'd have me drive them around country roads after things closed down so they could be together. I thought that made her happy.

I was so drawn into these scenes my ears were ringing and I sat motionless. Then a very loud song from a very tiny wren-like bird intersected my unreal world and drew my eyes upward. It sang its melody, then nibbled on berries just outside the window. It was mid-December. *Thank you God. Yahweh, my provider. Thank You.*

Mom's power fell to the ground like heavy chains cut free from my neck.

After this turning point, I discovered this truth:

She had owned my soul. She subdued me. But that day, I reclaimed my soul took Mom off the throne. I resolved to care for my little soul. My gut, my internal knowing, owns the truth that God loves and accepts me. And after multiple encounters, I know I don't have to perform to make God happy.

God's conduit people at the House of Prayer later said to me was "God wants you to know you are precious to him and he is pleased." Regardless of troubles, confusion, self-doubt, or guilt-shadowed mind. God's message consistently flowed with the idea of me being valued – flaws included.

Gatekeepers

When I first heard the term, I understood it to be a person who controls information or access to information. At the time, I worked as a job coach for a homeless mission organization. For two years between tutoring and teaching college, I worked with clients in career development. The final two months of a twelve month program focused on resumes and job search skills.

I was always looking for ways to address the wide variety of obstacles that might hinder the path to good employment. I found an interesting journal article from an equivalent mission in Canada that described gatekeepers in employment. An example of a gatekeeper might be a supervisor whose role is above you and would control communication between levels of the organization, assuring information pass through him or her before you. That's to be expected. However, if someone withholds information from subordinates and restricts access to normally accessible upper management, that withholding adds a sense of amplified power to their normal professional role.

Was I a gatekeeper? No, I delivered employment information to our clients at the most appropriate time. The eight-week course was designed to build and practice new skills, step by step achieving employment and developing solid careers. I didn't want to overwhelm or discourage these determined people. They moved forward in a strategic order.

The article was clear, and as a teacher, I knew curriculum had to be delivered in an order that allowed students to consume basic concepts before building more complex applications onto those basics. My course development was not gatekeeping, but as I read, I did realize a parallel.

The very first place in the bible that opened up my heart was the story that described fences, pastures, gates, and gatekeepers. I'm a livestock person from way back so I related well to the comparison. I went back to John to get a clearer understanding of gatekeepers.

John described gatekeepers' loyalties. Gatekeepers were more concerned about themselves than any sheep in the pen.

Maybe gatekeepers are a necessary role in the professional world, but there's no requirement for gatekeepers in Jesus' sheep world. Priests were the gatekeepers in the old religious culture; in this new culture, believers are priests.

It was only the good Shepherd who genuinely cared about the sheep. The Shepherd who would forfeit his life for the sheep. It was clear, by miracles, visions, messages from God, that the Shepherd could, and would, reach into my world and love me like no other.

I crossed a threshold, turned a corner; I didn't need any gatekeepers. I chose to disconnect from the power of gatekeepers. I knew they're not required for me to communicate with or connect to God. Nor did I require gatekeeper's approval to live a spiritual life.

At first, I was just thinking of fundamental religious leadership, but on the commute home from work that day, I realized I'd been living as if my mother and husband were gatekeepers. The husband I submitted to for over three decades, who was now divorcing me. The mother who still commanded me even over the phone. A light began to shine on other people still controlling my mind and my actions.

A particular scene in The Wizard of Oz came to mind. What's the difference between gatekeepers and impostor wizards? I'd believed in both for too long.

In the work world, I'm a strategic thinker. I need to know the vision or mission of an organization and I'll align my best effort with that strategy. But don't spoon-feed me a single task or single piece of data. I can't support a vision one datum at a time.

The husband preferred to manage me by veto. He'd delegate responsibilities to me, then not engage in any discussion about the issue – no preferences or limitations. After I began to carry out what he delegated, then he'd veto what he didn't like. I spent a lot of energy on trying to do the right thing only to get my legs knocked out from under me.

Same dynamic at church. Men were the gatekeepers in this institution. They wielded the power to open or close gates as they saw fit. No discussion, no obligation to explain. I saw no sense in the Church of Christ denomination gatekeeper roles, but I lived most of my married life believing someone smarter than me had figured out what worked best. I just needed to comply. I guess I was wrong about that too.

The Navy was less a gatekeeper than mom, spouse, or church. It functioned by a chain of command that made sense. A pathway of responsibilities and order. It functioned more like a fenced pasture for me. Navy boundaries

Released

were defined but the pasture was large. I could frolic like a calf, graze at leisure, and simply enjoy life inside the military corral. Not be focused on the fence but the provision within.

Gatekeepers aren't mean-spirited; it's just who they are. I did not knowingly sign up for gatekeepers. I didn't realize my mother was one, or that my husband was one, or that I could love God without the ones at church.

Now I truly know I'm in open abundant pasture, guided by the voice of the Shepherd whose voice overrules all other voices. Who knows all, past, future, and present and cares for my soul like no other.

Chapter 16: Peace Talks

He'd been sitting in the recliner watching TV since he retired four years ago. I came home from class one afternoon in May, went downstairs to greet him and noticed one corner of the beige carpet looked much darker.

"The carpet over here is wet. Did you see this?" I asked.

"Yeah."

"How long has it been wet?" Counting back to the last rain day.

"A couple months, maybe three."

I went ballistic. I remember swinging my arms like a windmill and yelling, "You're a lazy jackass! You've known about this for three months and sat here?"

He just looked past me at the TV. No words. No eye contact. No movement.

I remember crying and yelling at the same time, "I can't take it anymore! You better leave or someone might get killed, me or you!"

He left to stay with his parents a few blocks away. I still saw him when we worked with the kids to fix up the house they bought. He got a sliver in his eye one of those days and called to see if I could get it out. I did. We talked a bit, nothing deep or restorative. God had softened me so I told him it would be okay if he came back home.

Peace Talks

We agreed to talk. He agreed to listen to me. That had never happened before. We agreed not to discuss our issues with the kids.

We talked at the house some, sitting on the same couch but a couple feet apart, as usual. I thought it might be better if we walked outside on a trail nearby. New scenery, new hope.

He seems to want to work things out, reconcile, but whenever we debriefed one of the 'walk and talk' conversation sessions, he didn't – even just a few minutes later – remember the conversation or subjects we covered.

He got the flu so the conversations went on hold for a week. I am paying attention to him, helping him with food and medicine, but I wondered if there was something else I needed to be doing? I was still believing reconciliation was possible; we both believed in God after all.

One four-hour conversation to straighten all this out in three weeks' time span? I don't know what a standard of progress might be. I'm still watching for hope, praying about what I should be doing while I'm waiting. Maybe I shouldn't be waiting for him to say something. Then again, when has that ever worked?

He left for good on our thirty-ninth anniversary. (I'm pretty sure he didn't remember that was a significant date.) He left no note but texted me two days later: *I'll be at Rosewood until further notice.* Rosewood was an empty house in the country that his financial advisor and choir friend, Ann, operated at a retreat venue.

Over the next year, he filed for divorce. It was always a sin in his religion, until now.

I asked to meet for coffee. He replied, "No thank you." Find out he was seeing a lady he'd known from church for five years and having dinners with our best friends – ex-best friends.

My daughter wrote long email letters that ripped me apart. Our relationship must be demolished and I couldn't have the granddaughters over to the house anymore. They'd be moving to Minnesota because the girls sense the bad vibe between Dad and me.

My son tells me he is censoring me from his family. He glares at me when I go over there to help with the remodel of the house.

I thought we'd agreed to keep our issues to ourselves, but I don't know how they are treating me so differently unless he's talking. I found out later when they told me I verbally abused him.

He filed divorce papers anyway. Had texting conversations with someone while we were exchanging pleasantries in the elevator.

"Can you tell me what's working for you since you've been gone? You seem to be happy."

"I'm not happy. Too much has gone on. This will never be really happy."

The divorce process we agreed on was described as collaborative. We met around a conference table with our respective lawyers, a financial specialist and a family counselor. I hoped this would keep the beautiful family together even though the parents moved apart. We'd always been better friends than spouses anyway.

It didn't work.

PART THREE: PEACE IN THE PASTURE

Chapter 17: Quantum Reality

As I learn about drones, satellites, global threats, I keep in mind the Almighty Deity is bigger than all that. God encompasses all of it, like Sphere. When I hear people say "God is in control" I can't agree wholehearted so I tweak what that means to me individually. God is light. God is omnipotent. God is good. God is merciful. God is a positive energy field and a mystery.

...and personal.

I've tasted Gods' deep involvement in my personal history. I accepted the intelligent wisdom that rocked my world and provided me with hope and life. I relate it to the number line from middle school math. I'm much more to the positive side of zero than a few years ago and headed on my vector toward peace and joy infinity. Because I chose, step by step, to believe in the positive God and engage with the brilliant Holy Spirit of Truth.

I connected with a quantum kingdom reality, and intend to keep living according to the physics of the heavenly realm more than the physics of this physical universe. I want to mature in that atmosphere of love. Love is the energy in God's dimension. I have to breathe it in and exhale, letting love become my DNA.

I go to a biker bar often after church services on Sunday afternoon. They host a blues jam with some of the best musical talent in the region. I drink beer, eat tacos, dance a little, but mostly love. I see love, feel love. People around me have been hurt and twisted up in life. They've been hurt, hurt others, or hurt themselves. These are people. People with the same potential as people who sat beside me in the pews earlier. Same potential for meanness, for honesty and dishonesty. Same potential for love and hate.

It's not my concern to measure, compare, or judge. My business is to live as deeply as I can in what I believe about God. God engaged me lovingly while in my mess. Jesus demonstrated how intense he loved his father God by how completely he chose to obey. He opened himself up to be humiliated by mean stupid people who are all loved by God.

It is my concern to believe what I've witnessed and experienced. I read a section in John's eleventh chapter that made my position clear. He'd been doing miracles so people would believe him for over three years: feeding thousands, healing sick and blind people, explaining God.

He came to this family who were his close followers to raise the brother Lazarus from being dead. They were all crying. They confronted him about being too late to heal the brother-friend while he was still alive. He confronted them back, repeating what he told them all along about eternal life.

Then I saw this closer. Jesus looked around at the crowd of sympathizers, the sisters, his close friends whom appeared to believe, and – in his anger – cried. I can imagine how frustrated he must have been, giving his all to them, to everyone as God led him to, and this bunch still didn't believe him!

He cried, not from empathy for the mourners, but from his own disheartening realization of the lack of belief after all he'd done.

Quantum Reality

In one version it says he looked hard in Martha's eyes and said, "Didn't I tell you if you believed…" then he said to God, "…for the sake of these people so they will believe…"

I determine to never be a person who discounts or diminishes any of the strange wonders I've witnessed. They verified and clarified who God is and who God knows me to be. My main job is to believe. Jesus did miracles to show God's heart toward people. God's communicated his heart toward me via the Holy Spirit when I so desperately needed that heart.

I've written them all down, each moment, each event, so I can read and remember. But I want to do more. I want to practice the new truth that came from those turning points. I want to walk that truth out, that dynamic true wisdom that is alive and invisible.

What I now know to be true:

At each moment of these encounters with God, whether the message was visual or audible, whether it came from YAHWEH himself or through another person by way of Holy Spirit, I believed.

The messages were so intimate and clear, so precise. Their precision dealt with all the aspects of the particular situation in lightning strike time. Wisdom. No confusion. Nothing to challenge or doubt.

Like this morning. I'd gone to bed still mulling over how to describe this relationship between God and me now. These pages told of about seven years of strange spiritual encounters. How have they altered life? Got no direction that late hour.

Then, early this morning, as I shuffled down the hall, bumping into walls on my way to make coffee. Only coffee and porch swing on my mind. Before I even got to the kitchen, a song flowed into my mind. Pouring water in the coffee pot's reservoir, the words found their way to my throat.

"It's almost like falling in love….a smile on my face for the whole human race…"

Turn & Walk

Wow. A tender wave of joy and affection flushes through my soul. A Mona Lisa smile - evidence of my love for my Maker-husband who loves me. I sang stronger, agreeing with the Truth.

This single line of an old song describes God's perspective of our relationship, and now, my own clear paradigm. I looked up the complete lyrics online later and though it's a Sinatra tune, I feel sure these song lyrics were a message from God. I have no doubt God wants me to describe our relationship this way. It's how He defines it. He just told me.

Chapter 18: Hawk's View

Cut Off

We had engaged in 'peace talks' - sort of – that failed. No plan of reconciliation, he wouldn't see the counselor with me, it seemed mostly an airing of grievances and denial so he declared he'd quit.

My baby brother, favorite aunt and uncle had died. One horrible loss after another, and the worst loss I could ever imagine was the loss of my family. The loss amplified as family memories replayed.

Easters: little ones waddling between bunches of lilies and nooks of trees, hunting eggs, squatting to pluck their multicolored treasures. I hear squealing, giggling, parent coaching, "Look over here! Do you see something blue?"

Fourth of July: my two grown sons as teens, lighting Roman candles, Black Cats, and spinners from dusk to dark.

Mothers' Day: when I bought that timber swing set from the neighbor. My sons, along with my son-in-law and a friend, each grabbed a leg and walked the whole piece a hundred yards to its new home. Swings, rings, and a slide for five-and-counting grandkids. It was the first place they ran to when they arrived for sleepovers.

It's unused now. I haven't been allowed to hug or touch those babies' faces for months. They had their own daycare here – in this home, this yard - now just silence.

Turn & Walk

I try not to replay the audio of the kids' words but I feel their venom. "Fed up with your scowl," "we won't tolerate your excuses," "our relationship has to be demolished," "I'm censoring you from my family." I see the anger on their faces. I feel my heart tear.

The worst pain in my life has been the result of loving people. I remember what I read in Hinds' Feet. Much Afraid had to pull the thorned stem of a plant called Love of Man out of her own heart. This scenario must be what the author had in mind.

I'd considered taking the shortcut to heaven other times of intense emotional pain. Came close to driving the car off a cliff a few times during so many miserable years. But I couldn't abandon my kids. Now they abandoned me?

I know he did something. We'd agreed to keep our marital issues just between ourselves. I'm sure he's talked to the kids. To his parents and to church friends; I see it in their eyes. But I can't guess what he might have said.

He barely talked to me at all over our married years. Not about my brother's death. Not about surprise grandchildren. Not once during the four months I stayed in Arizona with my aunt assisting her hospice care. For three decades, he only talked of weather, nothing more.

But he's talking to someone now. When he came to the house to get a wall hanging of himself in his Navy uniform, I asked if we could go for coffee. He checked his phone texts before replying, "No thank you."

This is the worst pain I can imagine: my family gone. My cheeks are wet and my throat tight with a cry, but something's different. I can't set aside the amazing things God has said and done – to me during these same terrible years of loss. I have experienced God and witnessed His involvement in my life.

I saw an image of a huge tree stump cut clean, nearly down to ground level. I saw new shoots growing from the roots' perimeter. I heard a voice say "you must be cut off" with that vision.

I recalled the prophecy last March that God held my faith precious, like a parent holds the brass booties of an infant as a fond keepsake, but wants me to go deeper in my faith. I kind of knew at that time 'deeper in faith' probably included silence and trouble. Well, here it is.

Last week, I heard a woman named Grace, say "You are being stripped of everything you base your identity on."

Grace didn't know what was happening in my life. I'd never met her before. She didn't say who was doing the stripping. I know now that 'who' isn't important or relevant.

When the people who prophesied told me someone was shooting arrows in my back, they didn't indicate blame on any person. When they told me an adversary was lying about me, they didn't say it was my spouse. They did say "He won't be around long." They suggested I read Psalms 37 for hope.

Yes, the pain was deep, but so was the truth that there is a bigger picture I can't see or comprehend.

I recalled the dream where I climbed along a narrow mountain trail holding hands with two faceless hooded companions. I found out later those companions' names were Solitude and Sorrow and they'll be my companions on many more journeys.

As I stood there, I realized I had put my family between myself and God. God had tutored me, heard my cries, and loved me through this mess of intense pain and fear. God has not condemned, shunned, or punished me. If I put God first, there can always be hope.

I don't know how this will play out but I know God knows me. He wants good to win out, and has proven to me He can be trusted. It's my turn to walk that trust out.

Passing the Peace Test

1:30 a.m. My second trip out to Washington in the last month. Flew to Spokane, rented a car, and drove three hours in the dark on strange desolate roads. Night shift staff buzzed me in. Mom had a major stroke May 7th and was transferred here three days later.

I tiptoed in the room. A dim light was on over an empty recliner.

"Hi Mom."

"Carol?"

"Yeah. I just got here."

"You came."

"I always do."

I move close to her bedside.

"The food here tastes like sh__." She slurred her complaint without opening her eyes. "And the water is thick like paste."

I talked to Bob later that morning when he drove the hour in to spend the day. He was worried and a bit overwhelmed. His son and daughter-in-law were on their way from New Mexico to stay for "as long as it takes." He doesn't need to be driving that long road. I'll stay in her room here.

The third day, a girl asked, "How long will you be with us?"

"For the duration." She and I both knew what I meant. Later, chattering nursing staff moved a couch in in place of the recliner and gave me blankets and a pillow.

I held her water glass when she wanted a drink. Explained why it had to be thickened when she cussed at it. I watched her breathe – and not breathe. I heard her complaints about people not letting her sleep. I watched her sleep. Listened to her plans to have Bob build her a blue and white bathroom when she gets out of this 'goddam' place.

The physical therapy guy came to help her with range of motion exercises.

"She almost knocked me out last time. Her good leg must have had a spasm."

"Probably not." I said. He looked at me and smiled. Whenever someone moved her or tried to help with bedding or drink, she clenched her good hand into a tight fist. She pulled at her gown, threw her pillow, wagged her good leg, slapped her paralyzed one. I don't know if she was in some kind of pain or just wanted some attention.

I stayed close to her incapacitated limbs. I rubbed her feet with lotion. She liked that.

Toward the end, I sang *Tiny Bubbles* to her. She quit shaking. I figured it was safe to sing other songs, for me. *Holy Spirit You are Welcome Here*. I prayed.

What Lord? I know you are in this room. Let Your living waters flow through me. Help me remember when haters reject me, you've been through it too. I don't know how to pray for my mom Lord. You know her meanness, her arrogance. Why did she always have to fight?

She died eight days after I arrived. I left the building only after the cremation people rolled her away for the drive to Yakima. Bob didn't want her ashes so I had them sent to the National Cemetery in Kansas where she wanted to be buried. I put her beautiful cherry urn in the hole.

I did my best for her to the end. My love was still there. But she didn't own me anymore. At ages 85 and 65, she no longer had the power of a god or a gatekeeper over me. I only have one God now, and it's not Mom. I did what I did for her from my own love of the One whose self-sacrifice I honor and value. I served how I served to the best of my understanding of what a loving Yahweh conveys to me.

What About Him?

I asked God about that. I'd learned that God didn't take sides, like I didn't take sides in the animal world. I recalled a situation when I raised chickens. One barred rock had picked most of the feathers off another's head. Poor thing was bleeding and couldn't get away.

"Stop picking on your sister!"

As those words passed my own lips, I realized pecking is what chickens do. Did I love that chicken who was hurting the other chicken any less? No. Did I try to intervene? Yes. But in the end, chickens will be chickens. Skunks will be skunks. Humans will be humans.

I also had come to accept the idea that both Larry and I really had tried to do right. He couldn't be a different person than what he was. He valued being a nice guy and polite church-goer.

Just because I expected growth and needed more than he could give doesn't mean one was right and the other wrong.

God had also shown me a vision of the word forgive. The Source of forgiveness beamed forgiving light down from above into an opening in my roof, then that light radiated out porous walls of me, the lighthouse. New truth I embraced.

God spoke to me when I asked the question. He said, "Show mercy."

That's it. Simple and clear.

...and I wrote this:

Forgive "for the sake of Me" He whispers
Bear the pain of their shun
Be not tied or trapped in time
History is far from finished
Give them time to think and wonder
Their trials will come too
Life is hard with rush and cold
Be gentle
Grace and love to You.

Strong Family

Crying after my son told me he was censoring me from his family, crying to god that "all I ever wanted and worked for was a strong family..."

In a split second, the Holy Spirit spoke the truth and popped three distinct images in front of my eyes.

"You have a strong family."

I heard that loud and clear. I'd been crying loudly, you can do that when you're in an empty house, and this voice was louder and crisp, almost curt.

The images were groupings of my three adult children's family units, one after another. I saw each grouped as distinct units: father, mother, and their children.

Turn & Walk

I couldn't protest the images just shown to me. In worldly terms, I suppose each family unit has some sort of flaw, but imperfections were not addressed in that flash-truth. And that flash-truth became my new reality.

God told me I DID have a strong family. Not past tense. Present tense. It just didn't look like I might reasonably expect it to, since I'm the one left out of the images. I had to shut my whining up and be grateful.

Chapter 19: Assent to Peace

"Rest in it"

I'd just finished going through the house – again – to make sure everything was ready for the photographer coming tomorrow. Following the staging professional's punch list, I'd hung a perfectly folded sky-blue towel in the sky-blue bathroom. Chocolate-brown towels in the beige bathroom. Lavender fragrance in the toilet water.

In the only furnished bedroom, white plastic blinds made in China replaced my homemade purple crepe curtains. Two pillows nearly the same size fit well into virgin shams that matched a too-small but precious bedspread I got when my aunt died. An off-white bed skirt fit *most* of the way around the box spring of my queen bed to cover the iron frame.

Let's call my home décor style eclectic. We'd moved nineteen times through four states following his work. Lived in dwellings increasing in size from a one-bedroom trailer house to this huge hostel type with five bedrooms and three bathrooms. Furnishings were collected over time, each item with its own story. I had to block out their history as I repurposed and purged these last weeks.

As I went through the house tackling the list, I realized it wasn't the physical work that was so hard. I realized I was saying goodbye.

Saying goodbye to the kitchen designed by me and built with income from my first full time job. It functioned perfectly for multiple cooks at Thanksgiving for years. I served crepes and waffles from the gas stovetop onto the waiting plates of wide-eyed little grand-girls.

Turn & Walk

I was supposed to remove all counter-top appliances. I did…except for my 30-year-old Kitchen Aide mixer. She had beat countless meringues, cakes, cookies, and frostings in her thirty years. I couldn't hide her, but sewed a pretty new cover.

I paused to rest, leaning on the doorway to the screened porch. November cool. Trees changing color. Recalling scenes and seasons of the last twenty-five years.

We moved here to finish raising the kids. For the first time, each kid got their own bedroom. My boys painted a three-point line on that concrete slab intended for a greenhouse. When my oldest son ran away from home at seventeen, he left the first fort he built when he was twelve with his little brother. The boys played explorers in that dribble of a creek in these woods. We learned about tick removal. My daughter's wedding shower was on that humid July grass.

I raised goats, chickens, and ducks on this place. I buried both of our dogs, our first pet goat, Mow, and other nameless precious creatures under *this* dirt.

I was saying goodbye to the screened porch. Facing north and the largest section of the acre of yard. From that old oak porch swing, I watched deer, foxes, raccoons, groundhogs, and stray tomcats strolling along that perimeter. From that porch swing, I watched and laughed as my kids and grandkids played baseball, Frisbee, volleyball, and set off fireworks. My daughter's first kiss was on this porch.

It was time to take the next step. I'd already purged pick-up loads of stuff saved for others: kids, friends, my own hopes. As I went downsizing through the house, I was saying goodbye to this family's history.

These last seven years had been incredibly painful. Peace talks had failed. The divorce was final eighteen months ago. He wouldn't be back, and his philosophy assured his own hands remained clean. Early on, I overheard him on the phone to his little brother, "give her enough rope, she'll hang herself." And to me, "you can't push a rope." Smiling with his Cheshire-cat

Peace

smile, he delivered stab after stab to my heart. The kids had made it clear they wouldn't be back either.

I said goodbye as I painted all walls beige. One narrow strip between the garage door and stairway to the basement had been designated early in 1989 to record names and dates as the kids grew taller and older. It also accumulated markers for two baby goats born in the garage, the cat, our schnauzer, along with in-laws and grandkids as they were added to family.

I took over twenty pictures of that six-inch wide strip, zooming in, zooming out before I laid the wet brush to it, bawling my eyes out. I felt like I was removing all evidence of our family.

But I'd done it.

God has asked me to do some hard things. I'd faced some terribly painful situations. This was one. Selling my home of 25 years. But I knew it was the right thing to do, to downsize to a smaller footprint. I'm only one person, and in ten years, my age and physical stamina will make it an even tougher challenge to keep up with the maintenance of the yard. Cutting down trees and splitting firewood will become overwhelming, yet I know my fixed income won't be enough to hire help.

I'll have to buy a small place with any equity remaining. Exchanging 3,600 square feet for about 900. *I'll make do.*

Again, standing in the doorway to the porch. *This place will be great for a large family.* I envision kids hanging from the rings of the swing set my own grandkids played on. *I'll leave the riding mower for the buyer. They'll need it.*

In that moment, I felt like Abraham when he prepared to sacrifice his son Isaac. I held this home place out with open palm, honestly offering it and my future life to God.

"What do you want me to do with this place?" I whispered. No tears in this moment. No sadness. As I'd done the work, tears would have filled buckets, but not now.

Turn & Walk

"What do you want me to do with this place?" I spoke aloud.

I didn't expect an audible. Maybe I was just posing a rhetorical question to see if I felt a sense of approval or condemnation. But I got an audible.

"Rest in it." Clear as a bell.

The concept of rest had never entered my mind. Wow. Rest in it? Rest in *this* house? This was God answering a spontaneous prayer.

I stood still, soaking in His words.

This time I *didn't* turn.

This time I *didn't* walk.

I simply felt --- peace.

AFTERWORD – STILL WALKING

In my late sixties, I'm most of the way through the labyrinth of this earthy life. Only a few more sections to walk, God knows how many. Many questions have been answered, some are still on the table or will remain mysterious.

How does God connect with me now? Love songs in the quiet mornings from within my mind. Dreams, but not all dreams. I'll ask what He wants me to take from a dream, what it applies to, and listen for His response. I still hear His audibles, but not as loud. Maybe He doesn't have to yell.

Mystery. In the middle of a moment, I'll have a vivid flashback. Maybe a recall of one of those turning-point visions, and I'll smile. He's interrupted the flow of life like a friend pointing out a feature of a road trip we took together. How cool is that?

How do I know it's God? God communicates in a powerful and direct manner. Which aspect of God is communicating? Maybe Holy Spirit. Maybe Jesus. Maybe and angel or some other sort of unseen essence or energy type that hasn't been described or defined. I choose to not assign limitations to an entity that's all-encompassing, so which aspect of Deity is irrelevant. God validated weird phenomena, miracles, by their precision, timing, clarity, and method.

Only the God that is Jesus' father because that is the supernatural system I am programmed for. Joseph Campbell explained it this way. "If your programming is in Apple language, go with that. If it's Windows, go with that language." My native language is earth science, rural nature, and Christianity. Medical, electrical, plumbing professionals speak in their professional jargon. It's their common language. I'm a dryland farm girl; I also bake and cook a lot. I explore supernatural matters by connecting them to what knowledge I have of nature and animals or to familiar processes in my kitchen.

A few supernatural concepts, kingdom for example, just have to remain mysterious. I have no frame of reference for kings. I did realize similarities between the biblical eternal kingdom and parallel dimensions quantum theorists try to explain. I hope I compared them adequately. It's still a mystery. I'm okay with that.

Some words and phrases I use describe biblical principles, but only as a starting point. It's much more valuable that weird and wonderful incidents accumulated one after another as I kept walking along that labyrinth path. My understanding and faith increased by actively responding to these wonders regardless of any word or verse matching chore. Incredible kindness delivered through incredible precision – that is how God rolls!

Which significant verses do I lean on for these beliefs? Years ago, I heard someone say there were two main approaches to develop faith in God. One is to read scripture first then apply it to life. The other is to experience life then go to scripture to find confirmation or justification of that experience. Neither of these describe my process, but probably included shades of both. However crazy and random these encounters happened, one new truth turned me toward the next. Like wayfinding, getting from point to point may not appear linear from ground level, but points visible from an overhead view, are important in the overall terrain. I had to learn to trust God's overhead view of my messy life and suspend my own evaluation.

In today's world, information overwhelm is common. I don't want to memorize the whole bible, word for word. I want to consume it in sections with clear themes that I can incorporate into my ordinary choices and

Afterword

decisions. A portable knowledge base that I relate to because I've experienced it and can continue to apply.

During these years, I house sat for people, cared for church benevolence deliveries, mowed the church lawn. I carried a heavy key ring with even more keyrings attached. As I purged and minimized after the divorce, I kept only keys I needed. In the process, I realized I had keys, valuable keys, whose function I'd forgotten. I don't want to do that. Keys unlock truth. I have precious keys to understanding spiritual things in my life now. I don't want to forget what they unlock in the caring for my soul. Centering prayer, singing, trekking mysterious trails, all opened doors to spiritual principles and transformed my character. Made it new. I don't want to accumulate so many keys I lose essential truth keys in clutter and chaos.

Prayer. Sometimes, I just stand, look out my screened porch door, and open my mind to God's access. Sometimes I rant and bawl. I sing. I pray via ink on paper. The mode I use to communicate does not limit God. My emphasis is on tuning my own spirit receiver to God's Spirit transmitter. I lean in, listen, and get in the mode of obedience, acceptance. Like a designated hitter in baseball, waiting for the coach's signal. Engaged and ready. Making sure I'm breathing an atmospheric Love.

Belief. After each labyrinth turn, my point of view transformed; I realized something to be true that I didn't know or believe before. My mind changed over these last fifteen years because I witnessed the truer character of God. Character traits discovered by walking through strange and wonderful personal experiences. Experiences that no one can take from me. I finally believe I am loved by Love.

Purpose. When I was wrestling with eliminating two of my three jobs in 2016, I asked God what I'd do with the extra time. He said, "Serve." No more than that. No amount of time, schedule of days, or target. And it wasn't my subconscious that said it. The language and tone were sweet and simple. No qualifiers, just BE in a mode of serving. That told me his mindset. In the book of Acts, it says David fulfilled his purpose for his times then died. I want that. I want to run my own race, fulfill God's intended purpose for my life.

What about death? What I do know is life here ends – every second. The system of eternal life, that weird principle of Kingdom physics where I can be in two places at one time, settles my worries about that. I'm choosing to believe what Jesus tried to explain to people In John 5. He volunteered to become a portal between this world and his other world. Whoever believes what He said about himself and God crosses over from death to eternal life when they believe. No caveat. Pretty simple.

Perspective. How do I walk out life now? I live in response to God's identity of me – who God thinks I am. Do I have a well-worn path of practice? No, but a well-tuned faith ear to the voice of my Great Shepherd. I trek this current reality hand in hand with Holy Spirit, relying on the invisible no matter the tension I feel.

When God told me to deal with The Main Thing on that dusky October drive, my teary reply was, "Why would I want to?" God said, "Because I'll be there with you this time." That was hard to hear, bit he proved himself to with me. God engulfs multiple parallel dimensions and dances in subatomic quark. I can persevere knowing He can be with me in any place of pain, lift my face, and heal my heart.

This book is memoir, my story of a particular season. What did other people observe during my journey? I don't really know. That's a problem. I'm usually misunderstood and usually misinterpret other people and situations. No one asked me why I did something or what I was thinking. Observers, it seems, assumed their own rationale was behind my action or inaction. I'm sure my own faults caused others pain. I believe God knows the truth of it all and neither adversary intended harm. I am grateful for Mercy.

During my transformation process, life was crazy painful. I stepped into an invisible labyrinth, found myself on an unexpected quest for God and truth, and discovered the essence of Love. I hope some reader some place steps out of their oppression and trusts their journey to freedom, joy, and peace.

LEXICON

A lexicon is a stock of terms used in a particular profession or subject. A vocabulary of industry-specific jargon. The intent of this lexicon is to remove the weight of fundamental religion from this memoir. In addition, it will describe some concepts and terms that came from wayfinding.

I came into the world with a western rural jargon closely tied to weather, dirt, and critter environments. Far too many years of religious jargon have intimidated and deflected my search for God.

It's important to me to describe vocabulary terms here in a way that opens up discussion, not closes it down. This journey was inclusive, not exclusive. No walls were built, no barbed wire fences built.

This book addresses the connection between science and spirit. Scientific terminology will lay alongside spiritual jargon and religious jargon.

Abide: position of living inside, to remain in its place. To sojourn. In the case of the Holy Spirit abiding in me, it's like a permanent house guest. Warmly welcomed to hang out in me for unlimited time.

Abracadabra: is from the Aramaic that Jesus spoke. It means when a spoken word changes to a physical thing. "I create as I speak."

Blessed: fortunate. Whatever that means. Other synonyms are lucky fortunate, privileged, and honored. They all apply to the situations and sensations I write about in this book.

Did I do anything to deserve what happened, or did I somehow earn the situation or sensation of being blessed. No. When I was blessed, it was a gift. Like a gentle kiss on my cheek from one of my grandchildren is a gift. Whether the blessing is personal or material or relational, they were all gifts. Another feature of the weird realm, that parallel dimension generally referred to as the kingdom of God.

<u>Dichotomy</u>, oxymoron, paradox, contradiction – odd opposites. One of the odd opposites I'd like to record is that for the last three months when I worked hardest on the marriage relationship, I actually felt more separated from God, but I never doubted he was there.

<u>Disfellowship:</u> an old fashioned cruel practice of shunning still done in fundamentally religious assemblies. Cutting people off from family and friends because they have not lived up to particular criteria defined by the cruel assembly.

<u>Gatekeeper</u>: a person who controls access to something or someone. Access to information or power is restricted or hidden by a gatekeeper to exert control over someone. Not a religious term that I was familiar with but a religious function I was all too familiar with.

<u>God</u> = this is not God's proper name. I don't know what that is or if we even need to know. YAHWEH was used in the Jerusalem Bible, Jehovah in another bible. Some modern translations use LORD for God's proper name and Lord in place for where our generation uses Sir. So far as I've read, God has at least sixteen names in the Bible, first and last name that describes how He functions. For instance, <u>Jehovah Ro'i</u> means <u>God Who Sees</u>. Kay Arthur wrote a good book about the names of God.

In this book, I'll use the word God. Such strange things happened, and many times I said, "weird God" did it. Complete respect intended, but weird was as accurate a term in the moment as miracle.

Lexicon

Grace: is the power to act. God's enabling action in my life that equipped me to do things I'm incapable of doing. I experienced grace in this dimension by tapping into God's dimension via Holy Spirit. I don't purchase grace, simply and humbly acknowledge the need and connect with The Source.

He, Him: I've found no evidence that God is gendered so do not believe God is gendered. If God is beyond description, then to assign gender is to attempt to conform God to our image. The German language assigns gender to doors and windows, chairs and refrigerators. Think about that.

When I joined the Navy, I felt comfortable as "one of the guys." When my mother called, "Boys, get in here now," I, a girl, ran to the house. I knew she meant us children. I wasn't offended. For the comfort of most readers, I choose to say He.

If you're not comfortable with He and Him, make a change according to your gendered or non-gendered preference. Just don't lose the point of the story. This adventure explores scientific theory, multiple and parallel dimensions, and an entity, Deity, that possesses personality.

Manifest: transformation from being invisible to being seen. Jesus did it when he said "abracadabra."

Minister: to give aid or service. See steward.

Miracle: something that happens contrary to or outside the normal and expected physical principles of the dimension we see as real. Maybe an instance where laws of a spiritual realm intersect with or insert spiritual physics into this physical world. All miracles are wonders and signs.

Perichoresis: describes a dance between the Father, Son and Holy Spirit, in which any one of them could assume the place of the godhead, but, in radical self-giving, they continue to dance to give that space to one of the other members. This seems like what church people historically called the trinity.

This dance metaphor works with the way I experienced Deity. I moved through this period of life by waltz, polka, or Western swing, SomeOne took the lead. This term helped me accept that whether Jesus, Yahweh, or Holy Spirit led, Deity was my trusted dance partner, whoever led in the moment.

Pray, Prayer: Some sort of attempt at communication with God. Not necessarily words or sentences. Could be singing, humming, silently listening, ranting, crying, or some other mode of expression. Awareness on the part of the human may or may not be part of the interactive communication experience. There were times when I only became aware I'd prayed days or weeks afterward. Those prayers were just a tiny, quiet, desperate hunger deep inside of me. I didn't know it, but God did.

Prophecy: Simply, this means to foretell, predict, or speak under inspiration. The idea that someone speaks under inspiration felt awkward wrong to me early on, but after several precise and surprising prophetic moments, I know it's just part of communicating.

As I learned more about quantum theory and multiple and parallel dimensions I came to understand there are places between the physical dimension and the spiritual dimension where the lining is thin. Places that some people can see through. At odd times, I've been one of those people.

Many times, especially during this season of coming apart, SomeOne from that dimension has communicated with me. Methods included daytime translucent visuals, wordless but colorful dreams in the night, and loud audible phrases. A voice, not my voice, not masculine or feminine, but a familiar voice.

People around me were inspired to deliver messages that predicted events and my involvement in them. Neither the person nor I had any knowledge of the actual future event or its importance, only the message sender could have.

I won't say these weird predictions were delivered with God's intention to build my faith, but they absolutely did.

Lexicon

Quantum leap: Frequency waves of two separate dimensions exist side by side. When the trough of one dimension is near a crest of another dimension, there's an opportunity for things to pop over that narrow gap.

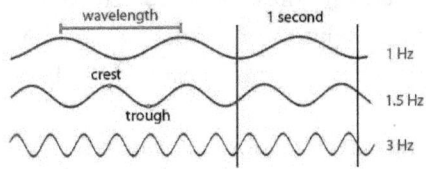

That may not be the way a scholar of quantum theory would explain it, but I'm using this example as a way to grasp the existence of heaven as a spirit dimension and earth as a physical dimension coexisting. I consider the physical world we live in to be one frequency and the spiritual world another frequency. The idea of Jesus as a portal between worlds is yet another epiphany of quantum theory principles.

Sacrifice: forsake. To give up something of value for the good of something of greater value. Higher value over another value is the point; both are valued.

Scripture: Most people will probably assume the word scripture is a synonym for bible. I'm not limiting that definition in this book. Scripture here will include the bible, but will also include the Nag Hammadi scriptures. I haven't seen the Dead Sea Scrolls but I won't limit the power of Jehovah to only preserved inspired texts. And I certainly don't hold tightly to the idea that the committee that decided for or against scriptures to be 'canonized" should be the end-all authority.

Spirit, spirit: if it's capitalized, it means a sort of wind, energy power that's an aspect of God. Jesus said to his believing followers that he'd replace himself with Holy Spirit and it would abide in them.

As humans, we have an aspect of spirit aside from that one, before we get that one. I spent a long time sorting through words like spirit, soul, and mind. I'd rather dance through life with them all than cut them apart from one another. Life is not about parts of me anyway.

Steward: to manage care. To care for something I don't own.

<u>Testimony</u>: means telling about those incidents, moments, and phenomena that I witnessed. I promise this testimony is an accurate testimony. I'm the expert with the experience here. God or Holy Spirit giving me those visions is my authority, my expertise. I'll offer testimony of accurate witness, word by word, dream by dream, vision by vision.

<u>True</u>: True means the actual state of affairs, essential reality. I built my version from statements and actions by other people, flawed persons I'd allowed to be my authority. During the process of this journey, I came to accept as true, weird experiences that didn't align with real things, events and facts within this world, but a reality of a different world, a spiritual world with quantum-like truth.

<u>Truth</u>: We look for the truth, the complete body of fundamental and overarching reality, to be absolutely perfect. I can't see any way to verify that some object or event perfectly aligns with that idea, especially because of my humanity offers only a partial point of view. I do seek truth, but know it can never be complete.

<u>Vision</u>: Something like a dream, but seen in awake times. Sort of translucent like what I consider a hologram. Visions are video messages from God mostly without words but sometimes tagged with an audible word like, "Generous."

<u>Wayfinding</u>: Finding out how to get from point to point without a map to guide. This can be in a geographic context, career planning context, or spiritual context. In this memoir, all these contexts presented.

I suppose wayfinding applies to any aspect of living that you or I have yet to experience. No matter how detailed or well-planned a procedural guide, it's impossible to see what's over the horizon before we travel there.

The concept is not the same as the experience of that concept. The map is not the territory.

<u>Witness</u>: To have seen. In this book, to witness also includes to hear and experience. I have witnessed love, betrayal, visions, dreams and daydreams.

Lexicon

I've witnessed strange connections between statements given to me by people and life events or conditions they know nothing about.

Witnessing compels testimony.

<u>Worship:</u> to give honor. It's a verb. Maybe it's singing. Maybe it's an existential verb like 'be' or 'am'. Maybe I can be in a condition of worshiping. Maybe it's praying, silently listening for God, and honoring God's awesomeness.

www.ingramcontent.com/pod-product-compliance
Lightning Source LLC
Chambersburg PA
CBHW052022290426
44112CB00014B/2335